Developing Multi-professional Teamwork for Integrated Children's Services

Research, Policy and Practice

Developing Multi-professional Teamwork for Integrated Children's Services

Research, Policy and Practice

Angela Anning, David Cottrell, Nick Frost,
Josephine Green and Mark Robinson

Open University Press

Open University Press
McGraw-Hill Education
McGraw-Hill House
Shoppenhangers Road
Maidenhead
Berkshire
England
SL6 2QL

email: enquiries@openup.co.uk
world wide web: www.openup.co.uk

and Two Penn Plaza, New York, NY 10121-2289, USA

First edition published 2006
First published in this second edition 2010

A catalogue record of this book is available from the British Library

ISBN 13: 978-0-335-23811-8 (pb)
ISBN 10: 0335238114 (pb)

Library of Congress Cataloging-in-Publication Data
CIP data applied for

Typeset by RefineCatch Limited, Bungay, Suffolk
Printed and bound in the UK by Bell and Bain Ltd, Glasgow

Mixed Sources
Product group from well-managed
forests and other controlled sources
www.fsc.org Cert no. TT-COC-002769
© 1996 Forest Stewardship Council

The McGraw·Hill Companies

Contents

Acknowledgements   vii

**Part 1: Researching and understanding multi-professional teams:
         working with children**   1

1 Working in a multi-professional world   3

2 Researching multi-professional teams   13

3 Organizing and managing multi-professional teams   27

Part 2: Working and learning in a multi-professional team   49

4 Multi-professional perspectives on childhood   51

5 Changing roles and responsibilities in multi-professional teams   60

6 Sharing knowledge in the multi-professional workplace   76

**Part 3: Planning, implementing and supporting
         multi-professional teams working with children**   87

7 Making it work 1 – addressing key dilemmas   89

8 Making it work 2 – strategies for decision-making and
   service delivery   102

9 Taking multi-professional practice forward   111

Appendix: Multi-agency team checklist   132
Bibliography   136
Index   143

Acknowledgements

We would like to thank the following people who have worked with us on this project: Bernice McBride, Sophie Weeks, Angela Jackman and Pam Irwin have all helped with the research process and in producing the final text. The Economic and Social Research Council (UK) provided the funding without which the research would not have been possible. We would like to thank the teams who allowed us to work with them and gain insights into their challenging and innovative workplaces.

We have taken the opportunity of producing the second edition to bring the policy context of our research up-to-date. The main thrust of our findings and argument, however, remains substantially the same.

Part 1
Researching and understanding multi-professional teams: working with children

Part 1 sets the scene for the book. It outlines the policy and workplace context for the study on which the book is based, describes the research methods we used and analyses the structure and management of some multi-professional teams.

1 Working in a multi-professional world

Policy

When we wrote the first edition of this book five years ago, the agenda for the reform of public sector services was in full swing. But there were always conflicting messages. On the one hand, the rhetoric of New Labour was to devolve decision-making about service delivery to local communities and to give greater choice to users. On the other hand, there was a proliferation of central government initiatives to impose systems of accountability on those delivering services, such as evidence of value for money and performance management against set targets and national indicators.

Underpinning the Blair government imperative to 'modernize' (DETR 1999) was suspicion of the power held by local government 'professionals' (and indeed by local politicians). The workforces in schools, hospitals, social care and crime control were criticized relentlessly in the tone and substance of government publications. The implications were that professionals were primarily concerned with defending their vested interests and were bedevilled by over-staffing, bureaucracy, duplication and time-wasting.

The barrage of negativity from central government was fuelled by intense media coverage of 'failures' in UK systems charged with educating, treating, supporting and controlling children and their families. Notable examples were high profile cases of child abuse where children had 'fallen through the net' of protection, accusations of low standards of literacy and numeracy in primary schools, and reports of the misuse of children's body parts without parental consent for medical research.

New Labour ideology acknowledged the interconnectedness of social and economic problems. In many ways, the 'Third Way' initiatives involving public sector service reforms reflected those begun during the previous Conservative Party decade based on the ideologies of 'market forces', 'value for money' and 'freedom of choice for consumers'. But the difference was that Thatcherism in the 1980s and 1990s was premised on non-intervention in family life, whereas Blairism was more paternalistic. For both parties, public sector reforms were as much political as practical. But had the Conservatives not achieved their political imperative of disempowering unions in the UK, it is unlikely that the public sector would have tolerated the radical and rapid changes in working contracts and conditions imposed subsequently by a Labour government. So the histories of successive government policies in the UK are intertwined.

Positive calls for interconnectedness and negative critiques of old-style public service monoliths generated a new mantra for policy-makers – 'joined-up working'. The idea was that 'joined-up working' or 'thinking' acknow-ledged the interrelatedness of children and family needs in the fields of health, education, social services, law enforcement, housing, employment and family support. The aim was to reshape services. The belief was that joined-up work-ing would make services more flexible, more responsive to local demographics and priorities, more efficient by reducing overlap of treatments, diagnoses and records, and ultimately more effective.

In particular, joined-up working was a central tenet of New Labour policy for reducing poverty and social exclusion. For example, the original construct of Sure Start, the New Labour flagship anti-poverty initiative launched in 1998 and costed at £1.4 billion over six years and a prime example of a socialist intervention initiative, was that all families with children aged under 4 in the 500 most deprived areas of England would be offered flexible, accessible, affordable 'joined-up services' (Glass 1999). The 'treatments' were to be nego-tiated with local communities and were to support them in escaping the pov-erty trap. Early reports from the National Evaluation of Sure Start (NESS) of the impact of the early intervention on child and family outcomes were disap-pointing (Belsky et al. 2007) and created sufficient panic in the government for them to unravel Sure Start Local Programmes (SSLPs) and rebrand (many of) them as Sure Start Children's Centres. (See www.ness.bbk.ac.uk for reports by the NESS team.) However, there was good news too. Some SSLPs were achieving better outcomes than others (Anning and Ball 2008) and the charac-teristics of these programmes were fed into the guidance notes for the Child-ren's Centres. As researchers would have predicted, by 2008 during which time children and their families in SSLP communities had been exposed to SSLP services for a substantial period, a variety of beneficial effects had been detected for children and their families when the children were 3 years old (NESS 2008). By this time the policy machinery had rolled on, leaving these encouraging findings buried in a plethora of new anti-poverty initiatives.

Throughout the decade of Labour government a raft of cross-departmental government papers were published to promote the implementation of inte-grated services. They culminated in the Green Paper, *Every Child Matters* (DfES 2003), *Every Child Matters: Change for Children* (DfES 2004) and the subsequent Children Act 2004, which built on the seminal Children Act of 1989. There were five outcomes for children and young people that embodied the principles central to the Children Act 2004 (www.dfes.gov.uk): being healthy, staying safe, enjoying and achieving, making a positive contribution and economic well-being. These five outcomes became a mantra for the delivery and inspection of services for children in England.

The Children Act 2004 required every local authority to appoint a senior officer responsible for coordinating children's services. Local authorities were charged with developing Children and Young People's Plans by 2006 and establishing Children's Trust arrangements for allocating funding streams to children's services by 2008. In the government documentation, 'childhood' encompassed all children from birth to the end of secondary school and the focus was on developing the integrated delivery of services. All agencies, including health, were to share information and assessment protocols and frameworks. They were to plan jointly funding streams and intervention strategies.

Children's Centres (initially in areas defined as deprived but eventually in every neighbourhood, giving a total of 3500 nationwide by 2010) were established as the base for the delivery of integrated services for children under school age and their families. Extended schools, both mainstream and special, were to serve as the hub of services for school-aged pupils and their parents. They were expected to provide: high-quality wraparound childcare before and after school, available 8 a.m.–6 p.m. all year; out of school activities such as drama, dance, sport, homework clubs, learning a foreign language, hobbies, business and enterprise opportunities, plus visits to galleries and museums; parenting support; referral to specialist support such as speech therapy or behaviour support; and family learning opportunities. Many schools are struggling to come to terms with this ambitious agenda. In 2008, *The 21st Century School: A Transformation in Education* (DCSF 2008c) reinforced the Every Child Matters agenda. Key principles were: powerful partnerships with parents, a resource for the whole community, promoting excellence in teaching and learning and 'narrowing the gap' between high and low attainments, and being at the centre of early intervention.

Meanwhile agency specific papers and guidance notes were also coming thick and fast, but embedded in all of them was the principle of agencies working together. For example, in Health, a National CAMHS review was instigated with the twin objectives of investigating what progress had been made since the publication of *The National Framework for Children, Young People and Maternity Services* (DfES/DoH 2004a) and *Every Child Matters* (DfES 2003), and suggesting practical solutions for delivering better outcomes and monitoring those solutions. The resulting report, *Children and Young People in Mind: The Final Report of the National CAMHS Review* (DCSF/DoH 2008), noted a 'sea change' in the development and delivery of services and significant progress, but also made a number of far-reaching recommendations for further work.

Specific recommendations addressed promoting understanding and involvement of young people and their parents and carers; better organization and integration of services to provide lead professionals as a main point of contact, clear signposting to specialist help, individualized and integrated care, effective transition to adult services and the establishment of a National Advisory Council, strengthening of the multi-agency national support programme and inclusion of emotional and mental health issues in core children's workforce training. Through the report there are references to the importance of emotional health being everybody's business and the need for agencies to work together.

Building on Lord Darzi's NHS Next Stage Review, *High Quality Care for All: NHS Next Stage Review, Final Report* (DoH, 2008b) and *The Children's Plan* (DCSF 2007a), the Department of Health and the Department of Children, Schools and Families published a child health strategy to improve health outcomes for all children. It is clear that the 'working together' agenda is still at the forefront of government thinking with explicit references throughout to partnership working between health, local councils and the voluntary sector. As well as specific policy recommendations for different groups (pregnancy and early years, school-aged children, young people, and children with acute or additional needs), the strategy makes recommendations about 'system-level transformation' concerning the strengthening of Children's Trust arrangements and cooperation and collaboration between agencies.

The Child Health Promotion Programme (CHPP) (DoH/DCSF 2008), also produced by the Department of Children, Schools and Families and the Department of Health, which focuses on pregnancy and the first five years of life, and *Child Health Strategy* (DoH 2008a) feed directly into *The Children's Plan* (DCSF 2007a).

Joint working is seen as a priority, for example: 'It is important that PCTs make use of children's trust arrangements to work closely with local authorities to jointly plan and commission services to deliver the CHPP locally' (2007a: 7). It goes on to outline a vision of 'integrated services' (2007a: 10) with Health Visitors leading multi-professional teams built across general practice and Sure Start children's centres.

In *Reaching Out: An Action Plan on Social Exclusion* (Cabinet Office September 2006), the government announced it would test the Family Nurse Partnership (FNP) model of intensive home visiting for vulnerable first-time young mothers. A total of £30 million has been allocated to support this over the spending review period from 2008/9 to 2010/11 and a randomized controlled trial has recently commenced. Although one of the FNP's goals is to link families into Sure Start Children's Centres, the FNP is an exception to the trend of encouraging multi-agency working. Rather it is aiming to produce highly trained Family Nurses, all of whom have a midwifery/nursing background, who have sufficient breadth and depth that they can deal with many issues without needing to refer on, thus reducing the number of people working with one family.

The Childcare Act in 2006 built on earlier commitments to expand child-care. Key drivers of the act were to improve the well-being of young children and to reduce child poverty and inequalities. Part-time free childcare/early education was offered to all 3- and 4-year-old children; and in 2008 the offer was extended in pilot projects to some 2-year-olds defined as 'vulnerable' and deemed as 'at risk' of low attainments at school entry.

In the field of child protection, the Children Act 1989 had already placed interagency work at the heart of the remit for social services. But it was in particular the Laming Report (Laming 2003) on the death of Victoria Climbié, a young girl whom 12 potential child protection interventions from different agencies had allegedly failed, that prompted the government to formalize procedures for moving towards the integration of children's services, with an aim of safeguarding children more effectively (Frost and Parton 2009). These arrangements were set out in the Children Act 2004 and its accompanying guidance. In November 2008, events surrounding the death of Baby Peter (initially known simply as 'Baby P') hit the headlines and had major ramifications for children's services. Lord Laming reported on the state of the safeguarding system following the death of Baby Peter in March 2009 (Laming 2009). This tragic child death led to reforms to the system of inspection, changes to the training of the social work and related professions and a government push towards further integration of children's services.

Yet despite all these well-intentioned policies, a UNICEF report (UNICEF 2007) on child well-being in the 21st richest countries in the world reported the UK as scoring the worst rates on five of the six dimensions of child well-being including child poverty, poorest health outcomes for young people (including early sex and high levels of teenage pregnancies and early 'risky behaviours' such as substance abuse) and lowest scores on children's assessments of their self-esteem. Perhaps in shocked reaction to these shameful findings, an ambitious 'Children's Plan' was published in late 2007 outlining 2020 goals for world class ambitions for all children, better support for parents and a new era for children's play and positive activities for young people.

Policy into practice: terminology

For those who struggled to design and deliver joined-up services, there was confusion both at conceptual and practical levels in the implementation of government reform of public services.

Epistemological confusions arose as the terms to describe different forms of joined-up thinking proliferated. In the 1990s, the talk was of 'partnerships' between agencies (see e.g. Jamieson and Owen 2000 and Frost 2005) and

20 years on the word came back into fashion (for example, the notion of partnership with parents implicit in the Children's Plan). Drawing on a review of research and policy Frost (2005: 13) suggested a hierarchy of terms to characterize a continuum in partnership:

- *Level 1*: cooperation – services work together toward consistent goals and complementary services, while maintaining their independence.
- *Level 2*: collaboration – services plan together and address issues of overlap, duplication and gaps in service provision towards common outcomes.
- *Level 3*: coordination – services work together in a planned and systematic manner towards shared and agreed goals.
- *Level 4*: merger/integration – different services become one organization in order to enhance service delivery.

The terms 'multi-agency' and 'multi-professional work' entered the discourse of policy and practice in children's services. Sometimes multi-agency teams were drawn together from distinct agencies for a set period of time and with an independent project or task focus, as, for example, in Sure Start local programme interventions. For Sure Start anti-poverty intervention programmes, workers such as health visitors, midwives, care workers, play therapists, librarians, teachers, psychologists, adult educators and counsellors were appointed. Some were seconded for part of their week from mainstream agencies. Others were appointed full-time for the contracted period of the Sure Start local programme. Alternatively, a multi-agency team operated under the umbrella of one main agency brought together to work as a team by systemic/structural changes of the host agency. Examples of such teams were child and adolescent mental health teams in health or youth offending teams in the youth justice field. Other groups of professionals came together as inter-agency teams for a particular case – for example, a child protection conference; or disparate professionals from different disciplines were drawn together regularly as intra-agency teams to review policies and practices in a particular field of work (Watson et al. 2002). An example is a group of inter-disciplinary health and medical professionals working on a rolling programme of planning services across a local authority for children with cancer.

As the joined-up working agenda became more established, the key concept became 'integration', a term which began to feature in the Every Child Matters agenda and was championed by the Children's Workforce Development Council (CWDC). Whatever the terminology used to describe their working principles and practices, teams delivering multi-agency services consist of personnel from a range of professional backgrounds. For professionals, a particular knowledge base, set of values, training and standing in the community at large give them a particular professional identity. Yet Frost (2001) argued that even the term 'professional' is problematic and fluid from a postmodern position where categorizations of professionalism are seen to be intricately linked to the use of knowledge and power in a changing world of work. However, we have chosen to use the term 'multi-professionalism' throughout this book as the most fitting construct to describe the coming together of workers from the traditional services for children of health, education, social services, crime reduction and family support into new configurations for delivering variations of joined-up services. As we will discuss in Chapter 3, the epistemological configuration of the multi-professional services on paper may seem to promise joined-up working, but it is the way the teams are organized and managed (from both within and outside the team) that dictates how effectively they are able to work together as multi-professional teams in practice.

Policy into practice: what works?

Increasingly, governments require public services to be closely monitored and evaluated so that any changes in practice are 'evidence-based'. The principle is that major programmes are phased in to allow time for testing, evaluating and, if necessary, adjusting. These procedures have been longer established and more widespread in the USA (Greenberg and Shroder 1997). A UK government review panel (Government Chief Social Researcher's Office 2005) argued that two types of pilot – impact pilots focused on measuring or assessing early outcomes, and process pilots focused on exploring methods of delivery and their cost effectiveness – are often blurred so that they seek to achieve both aims. The panel argued that evaluations are bedevilled by the complexity of what they are expected to deliver in terms of quick evidence of 'what works' in the social sciences. In reality, evaluations frequently become redundant before they have been allowed to run their course, as policy innovations at 'pilot' stages are quickly entrenched in government forward planning and political profile. Thus government claims of evidence-based reforms may be spurious (see Bilson 2005).

Findings of government-funded research into the effectiveness of reforms may be buried by delay or obfuscation. But one would hope at least that evaluations funded by taxpayers might serve to enlighten and inform the public about the complex and intractable problems of delivering effective services for a diverse, multi-layered population in the UK. As Young et al. (2002: 223) argued: 'Research can serve the public good just as effectively when it seeks to enlighten and inform in the interests of generating wider public debate. Not evidence-based policy, but a broader evidence-informed society is the appropriate aim.'

In fact, despite government enthusiasm for integrated services, we have little robust evidence of the impact of reshaping services on outcomes for service users. There is more evidence emerging of the impact of processes on professionals. But often professionals were directed to work in teams and expected to get on with it. Little training was offered to help teams to prepare for radical changes in their working practices. If we look across the evaluation reports of a range of programmes in the UK during the period of public sector reforms, we find common dilemmas reported in the processes of implementing integrated services. For example, early findings related to multi-professional teamwork related to Children's Funds (www.ne-cf.org.uk), Sure Start local programmes (www.ness.bbk.ac.uk) and meeting the needs of disabled children (Wheatley 2006) all reported common dilemmas: reconciling different professional beliefs and practices; managing workers on different payscales and with different conditions of work; combining funding streams from distinct agency budgets; and the lack of joint training and opportunities for professional development for both leaders and led within teams.

More recently two independent reviews of research in the field were commissioned (Atkinson et al. 2007 and Robinson et al. 2008). Evidence of the impact of reforms on service providers is growing. Benefits include opportunities for professional development and improved communication and information sharing between agencies. Drawing on activity theory, Warmington et al. (2004) argue that rather than rehearse time-consuming arguments about models of multi-agency work and their effectiveness, a more radical model might be to conceptualize loose, flexible arrangements of professional networks to collaborate on specific cases/problems in particular contexts at points of need. They refer to this construct as co-configuration. Benefits for service users are less well substantiated (Dartington Social Research Unit 2004), though it has been argued that integrated services improve accessibility, speed up referrals and reduce the stigma attached to services. The fact is that the jury is still out on the effectiveness of integrated services (see Special Issue, *Children and Society* 2009).

In this context of uncertainty about the benefits or drawbacks of multi-professional teamwork for children's services, we began the research project (the Multi-Agency Teamwork for Children's Services (MATCh) project) that formed the starting point for writing this book.

The MATCh project

The research was based at the University of Leeds, UK. An independent research council, the Economic and Social Research Council (ESRC) funded the project, so the research team were free from any constraints in publicizing the findings. The project took place over a two-year period in 2002–4. The aim of the research was to explore the daily realities of delivering public and voluntary sector services by multi-agency teamwork. We worked with five well-established multi-agency teams, exemplary of the type of team operating in health, the voluntary sector and social policy in the UK.

We were particularly interested in analysing the knowledge bases and practices that professionals brought to the teams from their previous work. We wanted to explore how professionals shared knowledge, how they designed together new ways of delivering services and how they developed through their working activities new forms of professional knowledge both as a team and as individuals. We wanted to understand more about how teams confronted and resolved conflicts in terms of the causes of problems and beliefs about appropriate treatments or solutions. Finally, we wanted to be able to provide exemplars of good practice to help other professionals working towards joined-up working. The research team was itself multi-professional and represented a range of disciplines. Between us we had extensive experience of the practicalities of working as teachers, social workers, doctors and psychologists. Our academic disciplines included education of young children, education of deaf children, social work, sociology, medicine and psychology. Thus in some ways we reflected the multi-disciplinary nature of the teams we researched.

Theoretical frameworks

The research drew on two theoretical frameworks: Wenger's 'communities of practice' and Engestrom's activity theory. We will explore aspects of these frameworks, as well as other theoretical underpinnings we found useful, throughout the book. However, below is a brief account of some key aspects of Wenger and Engestrom's theoretical models germane to our understanding of working in a multi-professional world.

In the field of sociocultural psychology, Wenger (1998) argues that new knowledge is created in 'communities of practice' by the complementary processes of participation and reification. 'Participation', according to Wenger, is the daily, situated interactions and shared experiences of members of the community working towards common goals. Reification is the explication of versions of knowledge into representations such as documentation or artefacts.

Wenger highlights the importance of professionals' constructions of their identities in shared practices and learning within multi-professional teams. Members of teams work together to develop a community of practice characterized by a shared history of learning and social relationships. The processes of developing a community of practice include mutual engagement (co-participation), a joint enterprise (shared accountability), and shared repertoire (common discourses and concepts). For Wenger, identity is 'a way of talking about how learning changes who we are and creates personal histories of becoming in the context of our communities' (1998: 5). 'Identity' is indeed one of four main organizing concepts in Wenger's model, underpinning workplace learning, alongside 'meaning', 'practice' and 'community'. Wenger views identity dynamically within communities of practice. Individual identity trajectories are negotiated (1998: 154) in activities in the world of work. However, Wenger's primary concern is the social influence of communities of practice on identity transformation. He writes: 'participation involves creating an identity of participation, identity is constituted through relations of participation' (1998: 56). Wenger does not make a distinction between self- and other-ascriptions of an individual's professional identity. Jenkins (2002) views these two dimensions as interrelated and intrinsically social. But Wenger's work can be used to make the point that experienced professionals in multi-agency teams will have undergone different historic processes of both self-determination and social determination of their professional identity.

We also drew on Engestrom's (1999) activity theory in the field of knowledge creation and exchange. An important premise in Engestrom's model is that conflict is inevitable as tasks are redefined, reassigned and redistributed within changing organizations and teams in the world of work. His premise is that such conflicts must be articulated and debated openly if progress is to be made towards creating new forms of knowledge and practice. Engestrom argues that change should be anchored *down* to actions that are 'real' within workplaces while being simultaneously connected *up* to a clear vision for the future. He describes 'expansive learning cycles' (Engestrom 2001) in the workplace as when communities/teams come together with different knowledge, expertise and histories to pursue a common goal. In order to effect change, they must work through processes of articulating differences, exploring alternatives, modelling solutions, examining an agreed model and implementing activities.

As we have pointed out, the project team brought different knowledge, expertise and histories to our common goal of research into multi-agency teamwork from the fields of health, medicine, psychology, education and social work. It was salutary for us to experience our own expansive learning cycles as we attempted to articulate and explore distinct approaches to conceptualizing practice, reconcile differences in research methodologies and reach agreement about the activities of communicating our new knowledge to audiences in oral and written versions. We will explore these tensions as we tell the story of the MATCh project.

Conclusion

In this chapter we presented the context for policy debates that led to a governmental focus on multi-professional teams to work with children and their families. We outlined two theoretical frameworks – those provided by 'communities of practice' and activity theory – that helped to inform our approach to the issues explored in this book. We have reported the broad aims of and rationale for our study. We now go on to describe the research methods adopted for the study.

2 Researching multi-professional teams

Introduction

There are a number of challenges to researching multi-professional teams. For example: Who should be studied? What aspects of their work? What sort of data should be collected? How should it be collected? These are basic questions of the sort that all researchers must address when planning a research study. To a large extent, those decisions depend on the precise nature of the research question. If, for example, we want to know whether multi-professional teams deliver services that are better or worse than other service providers, we would be interested primarily in *outcomes*. We would therefore need to find some proxy measure of 'quality' of service (e.g. re-offending rates for youth offending teams) and we would need to look at outcomes for a relatively large number of people, comparing those who had received services in different ways. We would probably also want to focus on the experiences of service recipients, perhaps with interviews or focus groups. These could also be outcome-focused (e.g. we could ask people to rate their satisfaction with the services received, or they could also be trying to understand process: what was it about the ways in which services were provided that made a difference?).

The questions being posed by our study were more concerned with process than with outcomes. Our goals were to understand the experiences of individuals working within multi-professional teams and the ways in which the teams themselves developed and functioned. This meant that our focus had to be on the professionals themselves, rather than on service recipients.

One of the goals of our study was to help practitioners coming together to work in multi-professional ways for the first time. Our assumption was that there were useful lessons to be learnt from multi-professional teams who are established and apparently successful. The purpose of this study was therefore to try and understand how such teams make joined-up services a reality and to look at some of the implications of this. Specifically, the research objectives were to do the following:

1   Collect evidence about how multi-professional teams work towards their common purpose of providing effective services for users.
2   Analyse which knowledge bases and practices professionals from a range of services bring to their new communities of practice.
3   Assess which new ways of working are emerging from the activity systems of the multi-professional teams.
4   Explore the impact of new ways of working on the participating professionals.
5   Consider the theoretical implications of the findings for conceptualizing good practice in multi-professional delivery of services in multi-professional teams.

These objectives determined our choice of methodology. We needed to devise methods which would allow us to explore the complex interplay of: (1) structural systems; (2) participants' experiences of knowledge redistribution; and (3) professional affiliations and personal feelings; in relation to evidence of (4), new ways of working. In addition, our data collection strategy was devised with an awareness of the need to minimize intrusion on team members.

The remainder of this chapter will present an account of the methods used in our study, putting this in the context of the many choices that we as researchers needed to make. Primary considerations were always a focus on the questions that we were trying to answer and respect for research participants. The challenge was therefore to devise methods which would yield the necessary information without being overly intrusive and onerous to participants. These considerations permeate the entire research process, not just the gathering of data, since we were always aware that the need to respect participants' anonymity could create dilemmas for us in reporting our findings.

Data collection methods

Documentary data

The first stage of data collection was to gather existing documents: terms of reference; agendas; minutes; annual plans; guidelines for practice; regulations; and induction packs. The collection of documentary data was seen as important for a variety of reasons. First, what is documented, and how, represents primary data about how a team functions. Second, it was a way for us to start to become acquainted with each team and its activities in a non-intrusive way. Third, from both theoretical and practical interest in workplace activity and learning we wanted to try and understand the interplay between documented rules and records and team members' participation in activities, applying the conceptual framework developed by Wenger: 'Participation and reification transform their relation; they do not translate into each other . . . participation and reification describe an interplay' (Wenger 1998: 68).

Observations of team meetings

Reading documents can tell us only so much about how a team functions. A team is made up of individuals and to understand how those individuals make up a team it is necessary to understand how they interact with each other. Team meetings offer the ideal opportunity to observe interactions between members and to gain insight into how decisions are reached and disagreements resolved. Team meetings are under-researched but they provide one of the few opportunities to see a team together as an ensemble. They are, furthermore, likely to be the major forum for interaction and decision-making. We thought it likely that these activities would be critical to a team's success. We therefore saw observation of team meetings as a key part of the data collection process.

One-to-one interviews

Documentation and observation of meetings would supply much of the basic information that we required. However, it was unlikely that these data sources would tell us very much about the team members as individuals: how they felt about their role and especially about issues to do with professional knowledge. One-to-one interviews were felt to be the most effective method for eliciting such information.

Critical incidents

The ways in which a team works are occasionally put to the test by specific 'critical incidents' or dilemmas. We were interested both in what sorts of incident caused problems for the team and in how team members worked together to resolve them. Given the relative rarity of these events, we could not guarantee that we would have the opportunity to observe them in team meetings. An alternative strategy was to ask team members to keep a 'critical incident' diary for a period of time. The diaries would give us information about the nature of dilemmas and how they were similar or different for different teams. They would, at best, only give us indirect information about how they were resolved. Our strategy to address this was to use the reported incidents as a basis for constructing fictionalized dilemmas for discussion with small focus groups from each team.

Choice of teams

Clearly the choice of teams for our study was important. Given the study objectives, we needed to recruit teams that we knew were well established with a comparatively stable workforce. We also had to be pragmatic. Despite our principle of minimizing the burden for participants, we were still going to be asking a lot of these individuals. We wanted to maximize the probability that the teams approached would agree to take part and that, having agreed, they would stay in the study. Putting ourselves in their shoes, we recognized that they would have to trust us and, in order to trust us, they would probably need to know at least one of us already. We therefore limited our list of potential teams to those with whom we had pre-existing links. Given the varied backgrounds of the research team (health, education and social work), this was not a major limitation. We then wanted to ensure that the teams that we approached would represent a range of different scenarios, for example, different lead agencies and different client groups. This produced a list of five teams. This was felt to be a maximum number for the level of in-depth study that we were proposing. All five teams were approached before submission of the funding application and all five agreed to take part at that stage. Because there is an inevitable time-lag between writing a funding application and starting the research, we expected that the teams' circumstances would change and that at least one or two would drop out. In fact, one team did consider withdrawing, but in the end all five remained in the study. Details of the five teams are given in Chapter 3.

Phases of the research

Phase 1

The teams were first approached when the tender was being prepared. They were re-contacted once funding had been confirmed. When the research fellow started, he contacted the teams to introduce himself and to obtain documentation. He arranged to attend a team meeting with each team, this time with another member of the research team. The rationale for this was twofold; first, to give a second perspective and, second, so that members of the research team could meet the participants and vice versa. We did this only for the second team meeting because we felt that two researchers attending the first meeting might seem intimidating.

Observation of interaction in group meetings is challenging, both ethically and practically. We made every effort to be unobtrusive at meetings, sitting slightly outside the main group if this was possible. The project team members gave consent for tape-recording individual interviews, but due to concerns about confidentiality, not for having meetings recorded. Detailed fieldnotes were made on the main topics, contours of discussion and decision-taking processes to record team members' participation in the workplace (daily situated interactions and shared experiences). To explore team interactions, the researchers drew seating plans (see Chapter 5, for an example) and diagrams showing turn-taking by different professionals during two episodes at each meeting. The researchers also collected meeting agendas, minutes and documents circulated as examples of reification (explications of professional knowledge in representations such as policy documents, team plans, minutes, rules and rituals).

The documents and fieldnotes were analysed thematically. From the fieldnotes, we noted key exchanges between participants and the diagrams showing interaction patterns gave us insights into patterns of dominance and dependence within key episodes of the teams' decision-making. Where such patterns were recurrent, this suggested they were significant. Our analysis of major content themes and of patterns of interaction was used to develop the interview topic schedule and inform the analysis of interviews at Phase 2. In particular, we explored the complex interplay of contextual/structural features of the teams (from document analysis) and the personal/professional dilemmas of the team members in generating new ways of working (from our observations and interviews).

Phase 2a: interviews

The second phase of data collection had two stages. Phase 2a consisted of individual face-to-face interviews with selected members of the teams. It was necessary to be selective both because of the limitations of our own time and resources and to reduce the burden on the teams. Interviewees were selected to represent both the different disciplines and the different levels of seniority within each team. Views of other team members were later represented in the research through their key incident memos and through the focus groups. A total of 30 individuals were selected for interview (see Table 2.1) and access was negotiated through team managers.

All those selected agreed to be interviewed, and signed informed consent forms. Twenty-two interviews were conducted by the research fellow and eight by other members of the research team. In the latter case, the research team member would already have met the interviewee at a team meeting. All interviews were conducted at the interviewee's place of work and at a time of their choosing. Interviews were tape-recorded, with consent, and transcribed in full. Every effort was made to limit the interviews to one hour.

Table 2.1   Interview participants

Team	Interview participants
Youth crime	A drugs worker, an education officer, a police officer, a probation officer, a nurse, a manager, a youth support worker, a social worker
Child mental health	A lead clinician, a manager, a senior child mental health practitioner, three child mental health practitioners
Special needs nursery	A team leader, a training and development officer, a special needs nursery nurse, a counsellor, a speech and language therapist
Neuro-rehabilitation	A teacher, a social worker, a doctor, a psychologist, an occupational therapist
Child development	A child psychologist, a health visitor, a special needs nursery nurse, a paediatrician, a physiotherapist, a social worker

Interview schedule

The semi-structured interview schedule was designed specifically to explore issues related to three main areas:

- interviewees' experiences of sharing their professional knowledge and skills;
- the ways in which their knowledge is deployed in everyday activities in their team;
- their perceptions of the constraints and affordances of operationalizing 'joined-up thinking'.

Although these broad areas had been identified before the study started, by conducting the interviews after Phase 1, we were able to ask much more focused and grounded questions. There was no necessity to spend time on much of the background and contextual data-gathering that would have been necessary if the interviews had been our first contact. Furthermore, the interviewer was not a complete stranger and was known to have basic contextual knowledge about the team. All this meant that we were able to make the most effective use of the time spent one-to-one with the interviewees.

Analysis of interviews

Interview analysis focused on team members' perceptions of:

- their professional knowledge and skills;
- how knowledge is redistributed;

- the constraints and affordances of deploying professional knowledge in service delivery.

The tape-recordings were transcribed and analysed systematically, using dimensional analysis (Shatzman 1991). Nvivo software was used to support the data analysis.

Analysis involved a number of stages (Strauss and Corbin 1998). First was 'familiarization', repeated reading and rereading of the transcripts to get an overall feel for the content. From this it was possible to identify the themes that were common across the interviews. There were two kinds of themes: (1) those that were inevitably there as a result of the interview structure (e.g. 'sharing knowledge'); and (2) those that could be identified as being additional to these arising from the way in which respondents had answered the questions. All the themes were then integrated into a coding structure which allowed thematic coding of all of the interviews. Once this had been done, it was possible to work with the coded data to develop ideas about how the themes linked together, and then to integrate them into thematic categories. This led on to interpreting the major themes: discerning patterns of meaning and explanatory concepts, and developing statements of relationships between influences, case incidents or patterns, and consequences.

'Generalization' was an ongoing aspect of the analysis. This meant ensuring that the themes and explanations that we were generating were not just one-off events and that they did provide an interpretative framework which was robust for the whole data set and beyond. This meant that the other data sources also had to be incorporated, and constant comparison of instances within and between phases was ongoing throughout. We paid particular attention to discrepancies and negative instances. Finally, we needed always to have our theoretical frameworks in mind and to reflect critically on how they did and did not fit with the empirical evidence.

Phase 2b: critical incident diaries

During Phase 2b all team members were asked to keep a critical incident diary. They were asked to record four or five examples of 'key episodes', occurring over three months. They were asked to describe key events, some positive and some challenging, involving issues of multi-agency team client-focused practice or knowledge-sharing, and not just incidents involving team meetings.

It was explained that the incidents would be used later in the project for the research team to develop invented vignette scenarios which teams would be invited to discuss in focus groups. Participants were assured that the diaries would be treated with absolute confidentiality.

Participants were given pro-formas for their diaries with the following headings:

- description of key event;
- date, place, who was involved, the history and build-up to the incident;
- your response;
- what you did immediately, and later;
- how the multi-agency team was involved;
- what team members and agencies were involved, what they did, immediately and later.

Eighty-one diaries were distributed and 30 different participants returned diaries. A total of 61 incidents were described. We identified the main themes in the diaries, considering only those incidents which conformed to our instructions to identify key episodes of multi-agency working. Many diaries did not describe specific incidents, while others did not describe incidents specifically relevant to multi-agency work. Eliminating those which did not conform, a total of 21 incidents were retained for analysis. From these 21, eliminating instances of repetition, 12 episodes were short-listed by two members of the research team to draw on as a basis for developing vignettes. After reading and discussing these episodes, the entire research team then identified the following major themes for development into vignette scenarios:

- dilemmas of induction into a new team and threats to professional identity;
- dilemmas of changes of working practices – confidentiality/information-sharing and workspace issues;
- dilemmas of teams as community of practice – membership defined by jargon – exclusion of incomers;
- dilemmas of liaison with professionals outside the team – inclusion;
- differing values of professionals and differing values of professionals and service users; implications for decision-making;
- dilemmas of devolving/mainstreaming of professional knowledge and skills.

Phase 3: focus groups

Six anonymized, fictional scenarios were constructed which drew directly on the themes identified in the diaries, and also indirectly on individual interviews. The six dilemmas concerned:

1   The tension between sharing expertise and acknowledging specialist expertise.

2   The reshaping of working practices, and negotiating a common way of working, with shared documentation.
3   Inclusion/exclusion of team members, for example, through the use of language within the team.
4   How you as a team would work to engage an external agency you feel is important to your core work.
5   How to resolve differences of values between team members and how to take account of the values of users.
6   Tensions arising from transferring skills to colleagues or users when people may feel short-changed by not accessing specialists.

Scenario 2.1

You are a psychologist working as part of a multi-agency team. One of the good things about your team is the way that everybody learns from everybody else so that you all broaden your skills. However, you are gradually becoming aware that there is a downside to this, which is that your colleagues no longer seem to recognize that you have specific expertise that they do not have. There has been discussion of a particular case that you consider requires specialist input from a psychologist, but your colleagues disagree and do not seem to feel that your view should have more weight than anybody else's. What do you do?

The dilemma here is the tension between sharing expertise and acknowledging specialist expertise.

Scenario 2.2

At your interview for joining the newly-established multi-agency team as a specialist in paediatrics, much was made of the need to respect individual expertise/knowledge but at the same time aiming towards common working practices in the delivery of services.

When you questioned the manager about how this worked, the answers were vague. When you take up the post three months later, you discover that the team buildings have been refurbished. You are to share a communal working space. Storage of files for service users is to take place in a general office. You feel strongly that you need individual work-space and are used to having your own room and your own secure filing system and storage of user records. You are very anxious about issues of ethics and confidentiality. How do you deal with this?

The dilemma here is the reshaping of working practices, and negotiating a common way of working, with shared documentation.

Scenario 2.3

A new counsellor has joined your very well-functioning, friendly multi-agency team, which works with troubled children and their parents. At team meetings and in one-to-one settings it has been noted that the counsellor uses a lot of counselling jargon in their everyday interactions. The counsellor quotes theorists and techniques which are unfamiliar to the rest of the team. The team manager has approached the counsellor informally and pointed out that the use of jargon is excluding the other members of the team. The use of jargon has continued despite this intervention. You suspect that the counsellor feels that they have a low status within the team and that they are using jargon in an attempt to project professional competence. How would you approach this issue?

The dilemma here concerns inclusion/exclusion of team members, for example, through the use of language within the team.

Scenario 2.4

Your multi-agency team includes health and social services professionals working together. You have become aware of weak links with education (not represented in the team). To strengthen links, you have started to invite a 'liaison' professional to attend alternate weekly meetings and to share some joint client assessment work. The meetings discuss criteria for making agency resources available to your client group (children with complex special needs). Concerns have been raised that some children fall through the net, and that the agency puts up barriers.

After three meetings, a colleague alerts your team to a pattern at the meetings of team members blaming problems on the new person's agency, and saying that 'education' is not cooperative. Also, the visitor soon begins coming less often. Off-record, colleagues said that the visitor (an educational psychologist) does not share the same communication style as the team. How do you maintain your team's identity, while nurturing closer links with professionals in agencies whose cultural values seem very different?

The dilemma here is how you as a team would work to engage an external agency you feel is important to your core work.

Scenario 2.5

A front-line family worker is aware of the clash of values between members of the multi-agency team for which she works. In discussions of cases, decisions about what services should be made available to users are hotly debated by those from former social services, health and education backgrounds. But a further clash of values is apparent when she deals directly with service users. She is currently worried about a case of a lone parent father of a 3-year-old with complex special needs. There are concerns about discipline techniques and an alleged lack of 'nurturing' warmth. Some team members have previously felt that formal action should be taken with social services, and others have felt that this would destroy the chance of working collaboratively to resolve the problems. How do you think the family worker can best voice her concern in dealing with different values:

1   Of the team members?
2   Of the parent in responding to the rights and needs of the child within a family unit?

The dilemma here concerns how to resolve differences of values between team members and how to take account of the values of users.

Scenario 2.6

It is part of your multi-agency team's philosophy to pass your skills on to professionals in other agencies. This is partly a workload issue.

You have been involved in a project training mentors in schools to carry out work with children 'at risk' of exclusion. In particular, you have provided basic-level family work skills to mentors who work alongside individual children. A confrontation has developed in one participating school. A small group of parents complained to the headteacher that mentors are 'not sufficiently qualified or skilled' to advise families on parenting skills. Now the head is threatening to withdraw from the project, despite service level agreements having been agreed with the local authority.

How do you resolve such problems that may arise from passing your skills to other professionals?

The dilemma here concerns tensions arising from transferring skills to colleagues or users when people may feel short-changed by not accessing specialists.

Five focus groups were established, that is one per team. We requested named individuals to attend these groups, selected either because we felt that their presence was key or because they had not been included in the individual interviews. In practice, not all of those invited to attend were able to do so. In most cases the group discussion took place with a reduced number of participants; in a small number of cases substitutions were made by the team manager. Participants are shown in Table 2.2.

Focus groups lasted for one hour and were all conducted by the research fellow and one other member of the research team. With participants' permission, all were tape-recorded and transcribed. Each focus group was offered three vignettes to discuss. These were chosen such that each scenario was discussed by at least two groups. The matching of scenarios to teams was on the basis of likely relevance but avoiding giving a team a scenario which closely resembled one described in a diary by a member of that team. Nevertheless, a number of participants greeted a scenario with cries of recognition, suggesting that we had been successful in identifying scenarios that had resonance for these team members.

Validation event

After completion of all data collection and analysis we organized a feedback event to which all teams were invited to send five members.

The day had a number of purposes:

- to inform team members of our findings and interpretations;

Table 2.2   Focus group participants

Team	Focus group participants
Youth crime	A drugs worker, an education officer, a team manager, a nurse, a probation officer, a youth support worker
Child mental health	A lead clinician, a manager, a senior child mental health practitioner, three child mental health practitioners
Special needs nursery	A training and development officer, a special needs nursery nurse, a portage home visitor, a special needs nursery coordinator, a speech and language therapist
Neuro-rehabilitation	A teacher, a physiotherapist, an occupational therapist
Child development	A paediatrician, a child psychologist, a physiotherapist, an occupational therapist, a special needs nursery nurse, a health visitor

- to seek their endorsement of our interpretations;
- to seek their endorsement of the ways in which we were using potentially identifying material;
- to allow them to discuss emerging issues with members of the other teams.

The emergent findings were presented to the representatives from the teams and their views and opinions were noted. In the event, the team representatives largely validated the data we had gathered and it was not necessary to make any alterations or changes in emphasis.

Ethics and confidentiality

Ethical approval to conduct the research was obtained from the local research ethics committee. Information sheets were provided to all team members and written consent was obtained prior to interviews and focus groups. Participants were assured of confidentiality and a writing protocol for publications was adopted to ensure this. Thus, throughout this book we have endeavoured to protect participants' identities by using a generic approach – for example, 'one of the social workers', 'one of the professionals', wherever this is possible and not necessarily identifying their team if this would be likely to lead to their identification.

The issue of identifiability was one that we specifically raised with participants at the final validation event. Those present not only endorsed our interpretation of our findings, but also assured us that they were happy with the ways in which we were using potentially identifying material.

'Reflective practice'

'Reflective practice' is nowadays urged on professionals of all disciplines. It had a particular meaning for us in carrying out this piece of research as we quickly realized that we were ourselves an example of that which we were studying. We not only had different professional training (teacher, social worker, doctor and psychologist) but had also had very different professional trajectories and allegiances. Although, at the time of carrying out the research, we were all employed by the same university, we were in different departments which had different cultures and management styles. This awareness of ourselves as a multi-agency team allowed us to add another level of iteration to our research; we were ourselves another source of data, a 'reality check' for our emerging theories. Conversely, awareness of issues which were challenges for us, for example, different approaches to 'confidentiality', sensitized us to look for parallels in the teams we were studying.

Conclusion

This chapter has outlined the issues that we had to address in deciding how to gather data to answer our study questions. Our goals were to understand the experiences of individuals working within multi-professional teams and the ways in which the teams themselves developed and functioned. This meant that our focus was on the professionals themselves, rather than on service recipients. Our methods were chosen to give us a multi-faceted picture of participants' experiences and perspectives while minimizing the burden on them. We therefore used existing documentation and observation of team meetings as well as interviews, critical incident diaries and focus groups. So much data could have been overwhelming, but we were able to make efficient use of it, especially with the help of the data management software, and could feel confident that we had enough different data sources to substantiate our analysis. Analysis was an iterative process whereby emergent themes were constantly tested against the data themselves and the theoretical frameworks within which we were working. Finally, we validated our findings by presenting them both to team members and to other professionals for discussion and endorsement.

Two particular aspects of our methods were somewhat unusual. First, we gained a great many valuable insights by observing team meetings. This is not a widely used means of gathering data, but was one that we found very rich and which had the major advantage of not taking up any extra time from team members. It was ideal for a study like ours that was focused on teams, because team meetings were often the only time that the team came together. These observations were also a very valuable prelude to the individual interviews, allowing us to make the best use of the interview itself to focus on issues specific to that individual. The other slightly unusual aspect of our methods was the use of vignettes in the focus groups. What was unusual was that the vignettes were developed from the team members' own 'critical incident' diaries, so that we could feel confident that we were presenting vignettes that were grounded in their own experiences. Not only did this prove to be an effective research tool, but this was an opportunity for reflection that the team members seemed to welcome. It may be that this technique has further potential as a way of helping team members to explore their attitudes and beliefs in a relatively unpressured setting.

3 Organizing and managing multi-professional teams

Introduction

In this chapter the functions and organizational structures of the five multi-professional teams participating in the MATCh research project will be outlined and analysed. Øvretveit (1993) examined multi-disciplinary teams working in adult mental health and as a result defined five organizational team types. This typology was helpful in our thinking about the organization of the teams in the study and we will apply it to them in this chapter. Figure 3.1 illustrates our thoughts on the different lines of accountability in multi-professional teams. The team types outlined by Øvretveit are as follows:

- *The fully managed team:* a team manager is accountable for all the management work and for the performance of all team members – see Figure 3.2.
- *The coordinated team:* one person takes on most of the management and coordination work but is not accountable for the clinical work of individual team members – see Figure 3.3.
- *The core and extended team:* the core team members are fully managed by the team leader with extended team members (usually part-time) remaining managed by their professional managers in their agency of origin – see Figure 3.4.

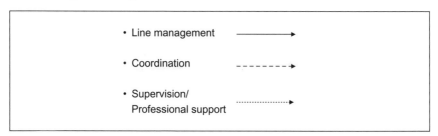

Figure 3.1 Key for lines of accountability

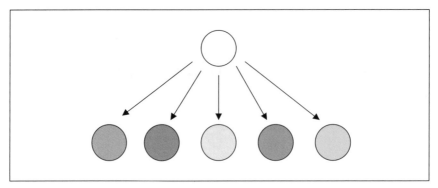

Figure 3.2 The fully managed team

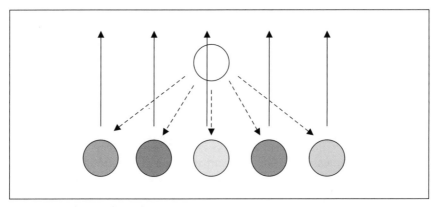

Figure 3.3 The coordinated team

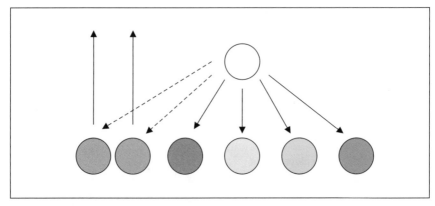

Figure 3.4 The core and extended team

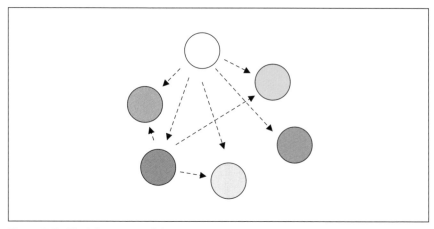

Figure 3.5   The joint accountability team

- *The joint accountability team:* most team tasks, including leadership, are undertaken by the team corporately, usually by delegating to individual members. Team members remain accountable to managers in their agencies of origin but in practice may not have strong management links with them – see Figure 3.5.
- *The network association:* this is not a 'formal' team as such but different professionals working with the same client or client group meet together based on a need to share common work/clinical interests. Each practitioner remains under the management of their own professional manager but decisions about client care are often formulated collectively at network meetings.

All of the teams were based in the same city, some covering the whole of the city (and one, the neuro-rehabilitation team, covering the wider region). Two of the teams (youth crime and young people) covered just a sector of the city. Thus, all five teams offered services to the same sector of the city although some offered services elsewhere as well. Given the government's strategic intention to integrate children's services, as we outlined in Chapter 1, it is therefore not surprising that in interviews team members from one team made reference to the work of other teams participating in the research. It is possible to imagine a family where a younger child with learning disability had been assessed by the child development team and attended the nursery and an older sibling who had suffered a head injury had behavioural problems, including offending behaviour that led to the involvement of the neuro-rehabilitation team, the young people's team and the youth crime team. Such a family would therefore have received services from all our teams.

The functions, locations, membership and organizational structures of the teams are summarized in Table 3.1.

Table 3.1 Summary of team function, location, membership and organizational structure

Team function and size	Client group	Base	Lead sector	Agencies represented	Agency stakeholder liaison	Team type
Youth crime team (13 members)	Youth crime, 10–17 years	Independent community	Legal/police	Health, social services, education, police/probation, voluntary sector	Yes, partnership group	Fully managed
Young people's team (11 members)	Emotional and behavioural problems, 0–17 years	Social services, community	Social services	Health, social services	Yes, strategic development group	Fully managed*
Nursery team (11 members)	Learning disability, 0–5 years	Independent, community	Voluntary sector	Health, voluntary sector	No	Core (fully managed) and extended
Head injury team (13 members)	Traumatic brain injury, 0–17 years	Health, hospital	Health	Health, social services, education	No	Network/joint accountability
Child development team (14 members)	Learning disability, 0–5 years	Health, hospital	Health	Health, social services	No	Core and extended/joint accountability

* With exception of consultant clinical psychologist

The youth crime team

National policy

The development of youth offending teams can be traced back to the publication of the Audit Commission report *Misspent Youth* (1996). This report highlighted the lack of joined-up thinking within the youth justice system as a whole and a consequent inefficient deployment of resources, and in particular delay in the processing of youth offenders within the criminal justice system. The Crime and Disorder Act (1998) paved the way for the establishment of youth offending teams, whose principal aim was to reduce youth offending by

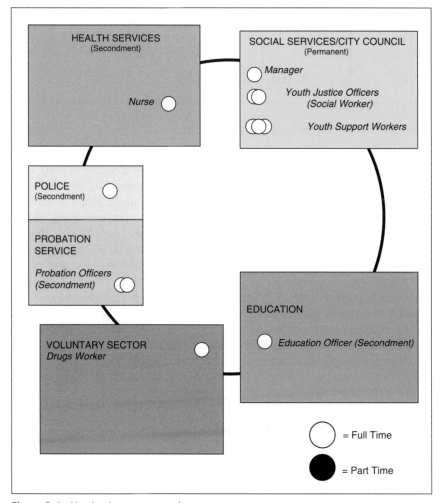

Figure 3.6 Youth crime team: employment structure

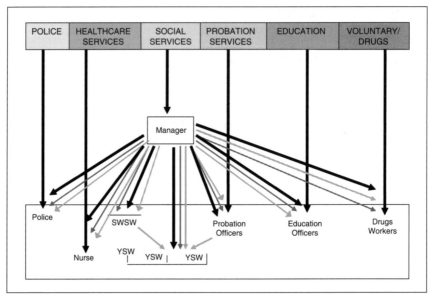

Figure 3.7   Youth crime team: management structure

children and young people (defined as those aged 10–17 years) in their area. The circular setting out the establishment of youth offending teams (Home Office 1998) specified that these teams should be multi-professional and should tackle factors associated with crime, such as poor parenting, abuse, mental health problems, truancy and substance misuse. The entire youth justice system was to be overseen by the Youth Justice Board, which sets the broad strategic and policy agenda for the youth justice system in England and Wales. The Act was fully implemented in April 2000. The teams, by statute, comprised at least one social worker, a probation officer and a police officer as well as persons nominated by the local health authority and local chief education officer. Funding for the team was from each of these agencies. In practice, teams tended to be larger and more multi-disciplinary than suggested by the statutory minimum. An Audit Commission report (2004) highlighted some of the ways in which the teams were operating well and also made suggestions to improve the functioning of the youth offending teams.

In 2009, the Youth Justice Board introduced 'The Scaled Approach' to youth justice which aimed to do the following:

- to develop a tiered approach to interventions in order to reduce likelihood of reoffending and risk of serious harm and that supports the introduction of a *new sentencing framework*;
- to ensure a coherent relationship between *National Standards for Youth*

Justice Services, Key Elements of Effective Practice and the new *Case Management Guidance;*

- to support case management as an end-to-end process, and improve practice in *assessment* completion, pre-sentence report (PSR) writing and intervention planning.

(see http://www.yjb.gov.uk/en-gb/practitioners/ youthjusticethescaledapproach/, accessed 1 August 2009)

Local practice

The team that participated in this research served an area of large estates of former state housing and back-to-back or terraced housing. There were considerable pockets of deprivation in the area. The population of the former state housing estates might be described as white working class, while the private housing areas were lived in by families who had their origins in Pakistan or Bangladesh.

The team was located in an office block just south of the city centre. All the staff were based together in a building which had facilities for hosting meetings. Staffing at the time of the research comprised a manager, two social workers (youth justice officers), two probation officers, a police officer, a drugs worker, an education officer, a nurse, three youth support workers and two administrative officers. Funding from agencies contributing to the team was in roughly the following proportions: social services, 55 per cent; probation, 20 per cent; police, 10 per cent; education, 10 per cent; and health, 5 per cent.

As shown in Figure 3.6 the team did not quite meet Øvretveit's (1993) criteria for a fully managed team. The manager, employed by social services, had line management responsibility for some aspects of staff employed by other agencies but team members still had functions line managed by managers within their original agencies. The team was probably best described as a coordinated team, with the team manager having clear responsibility for ensuring that work was allocated according to agreed priorities (see Figure 3.7). As with all the youth offending teams in the city, the team was coordinated by a partnership group allowing the stakeholder agencies to have regular oversight of the team functioning.

The young people's team

National policy

In the early 1990s, concerns about the ad hoc and uneven nature of mental health services for children and families led to the NHS Health Advisory Service (HAS) producing a thematic review, *Child & Adolescent Mental Health Services: Together We Stand* (NHS HAS 1995). The review described the state of services at the time and made comprehensive recommendations for

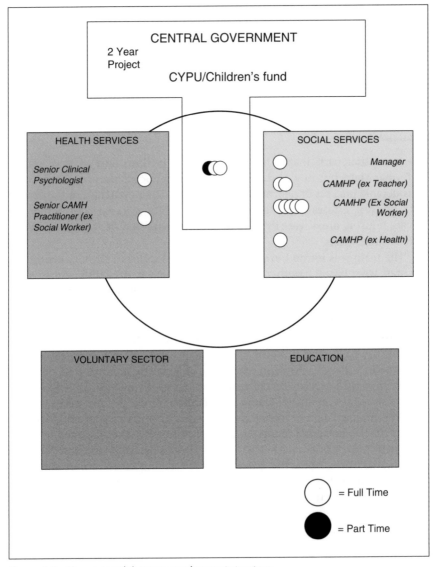

Figure 3.8 Young people's team: employment structure

purchasers and providers of child and adolescent mental health (CAMH) services. A major theme was the requirement for joint commissioning and delivery of services across agencies. The multi-factorial aetiology of childhood mental health problems was seen as necessitating the involvement of a range of professionals from different backgrounds and therefore the collaboration of a range of agencies from the statutory and voluntary sectors. Adequate mental

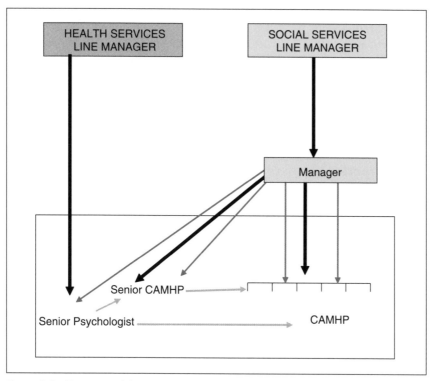

Figure 3.9   Young people's team: management structure

health services for young people were seen as having benefits for the future mental health of adults, but they would also impact on levels of child abuse, behaviour problems in schools, juvenile delinquency and family breakdown.

The HAS report proposed a tiered service model and was endorsed by the House of Commons Select Committee on Health in 1997. Tier 1 comprises front-line staff from a range of agencies (teachers, school nurses, general practitioners, health visitors, social workers, etc.) who have day-to-day contact with children with mental health problems but do not have specialist training in working with those problems. Tier 2 represents the first tier of specialist CAMH services. This comprises staff with specialist training in CAMH practice who, either singly or in teams, work in the community directly with children and families. They also provide consultation and training for Tier 1 staff to enable them to provide a better service for the children that they see on a daily basis. Tier 3 consists of teams of CAMH professionals working together to provide specialist interventions for complex problems. Tier 4 is the specialist provision of day and in-patient services.

Recent policy has reinforced the importance of multi-agency CAMH provision in the government's thinking about children's services (DfES/DoH 2004a). Multi-agency local delivery plans are now required to specify how improvements in CAMH services will be achieved and significant increases in expenditure are being delivered through local authority social services budgets as well as health, thus requiring health and social services to work together to deliver CAMH services. (For a history of CAMH services, see Cottrell and Kramm (2005). An account of Child and Adolescent Mental Health Services (2007) can be found at www.everychildmatters.gov.uk/health/camhs.)

Local practice

In the city where the MATCh project took place there were at that time five community-based Tier 2 CAMH teams, two funded and managed by social services, with the other three teams funded and managed by health. All five teams worked to an agreed service description with common referral pathways and intervention packages. The teams were locally based, worked closely with other statutory and voluntary sector organizations within the local community, and acted as a first point of contact for anyone concerned about emotional and behavioural problems in children. The teams offered clinical/therapeutic interventions with children and families. They provided consultation, supervision, and training to Tier 1 professionals. They filtered referrals of a more complex and persistent nature to the Tier 3/Tier 4 CAMH teams.

The CAMH team in the MATCh project was originally based within a health centre but had recently relocated to a jointly funded (health and local authority) one-stop children's centre nearby. The team shared a building with local social service and primary care staff.

The staff group comprised a part-time manager and 3.5 generic child and adolescent mental health practitioners (CAMHPs), all employed by social services. This practitioner grade was a new one created for the purposes of establishing the team and allowed for people with a range of professional backgrounds (nursing, social work, occupational therapy, etc.) to be employed by social services on a single grade. The manager had full line management responsibility for these staff. A part-time consultant clinical psychologist and a senior CAMHP were seconded to the team from health. In addition, two school-based CAMHPs had temporary funding from the local children's fund (see Figure 3.8).

The team functioned as a fully managed team (Øvretveit 1993), as shown in Figure 3.9, except that the psychologist, who was line managed through health, had responsibility for clinical supervision within the team.

The nursery team

National policy

In the 1970s, educational provision for young children with disabilities moved from a 'medical model' where children were frequently assigned to residential schools away from their families, to a special school model where children

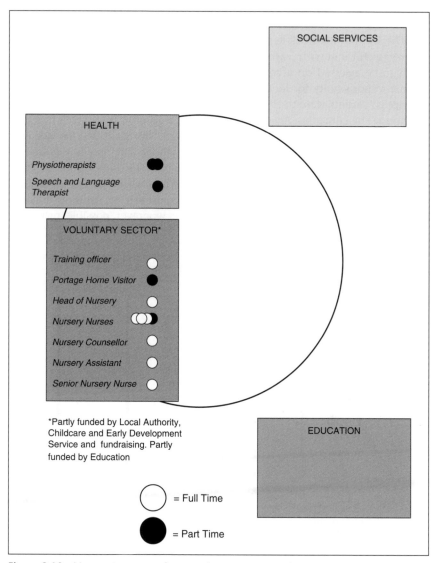

Figure 3.10 Nursery team: members employment structure*

were transported to local education authority provision. Special schools were categorized as for children with moderate, severe or severely subnormal learning difficulties. In the 1990s, there was a shift to an inclusion model where provision was within mainstream settings, sometimes as specialized units incorporated into primary school buildings. For children under 5, educational provision was incorporated into a diversity of settings: childcare, playgroups, nursery classes, nursery schools and children's centres. Some were financed by local authorities and others by commercial interests or the voluntary sector (Wall 2003).

The seminal Warnock Report (DES 1978) had argued for a commitment to educating children with learning difficulties as a matter of right and for their needs to be assessed on a continuum. Education rather than health was to assume responsibility for identifying and assessing young children with special needs. Parents were to be closely involved as partners in decisions about provision. The Education Act (1981) provided a legislative framework to reflect these principles. Subsequently, the Children Act 1989 identified the need for multi-disciplinary approaches to providing services. The *Special Educational Needs Code of Practice* (DfES 2001) re-emphasized the importance of early identification, diagnosis and provision for children with learning disabilities and the importance of a multi-disciplinary approach to decision-making. There was a strong message about inclusion: wherever possible provision

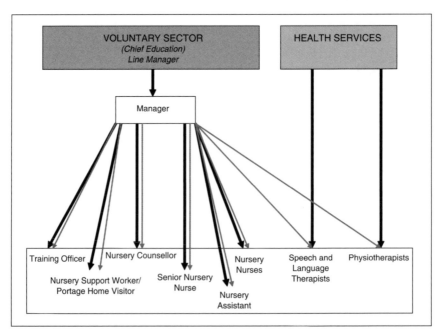

Figure 3.11   Nursery team: management structure

should be in mainstream settings. This resulted in a raft of special educational needs training for staff in mainstream pre-school and school settings, who were expected to respond to the needs of young children with a range of disabilities. In 2002, the Department for Education and Skills and Department of Health (2002a, 2002b) published guidelines for multi-agency working for the delivery of services to children with disabilities from birth to 2 and their families. Key messages in both documents were multi-agency assessment and decision-making, joint working, information-sharing and a child-centred approach to provision for young children with special needs. There was a pledge in the Children's Plan launched in 2007 that additional funding would be provided for children with Special Educational Needs and children with dyslexia.

Local practice

The nursery that participated in the research had opened in 1963 operating under the auspices of the Royal Society for Mentally Handicapped Children and Adults (MENCAP). It was based in their main headquarters in a converted nursery school building. The nursery was a registered charity and there was a small daily charge for children's attendance. The nursery ethos dominated the building. Seconded health workers had rooms allocated for one-to-one work with children and parents.

The nursery offered services to 40 children with learning disabilities, from birth to 4, and their families. Referrals came from a wide range of sources across the city. Many of the children had additional (some multiple and profound) disabilities: physical, sensory and behavioural as well as developmental delay. Following enrolment, parents and nursery workers completed an integrated assessment leading to an individual education plan for the child. Provision for children included play-based learning activities, physiotherapy, speech therapy and organized visits to the library, shops, parks, local leisure centres and museums/galleries. Adults were offered group parenting and support sessions, sometimes with visiting speakers, and individual advice and counselling sessions. Health workers provided direct work with children and parents but were increasingly expected to 'train' nursery staff in their specialist knowledge/expertise by modelling activities with children in the main classrooms. There was outreach work in family homes through the 'Portage' home visitor scheme. The training officer worked in a range of early years settings, mentoring mainstream staff in the skills and expertise of provision for young children with additional needs. Many of these initiatives were innovative in their time, and indeed the kinds of practices that were espoused by Sure Start Local Programmes in the first decade of the new millennium.

The staff group comprised a head of nursery, counsellor, senior nursery nurse, three nursery nurses, a nursery escort/assistant, an administrative assistant, an ethnic minority development worker, a minibus driver, cleaner and assistant cleaner, bookkeeper, fundraising and development manager and fundraiser as well as a Portage home visitor. Health staff with specific sessions allocated to the nursery included two part-time physiotherapists and one part-time speech therapist. In addition, a full-time training officer was funded by the local Early Years Development and Childcare Partnership (EYDCP), at that period the way in which funding was distributed to early years services within Local Authorities. There were also a range of voluntary workers contributing to cooking, driving and working with the children. Funding came from three main sources: grants from the local education authority and NHS, fundraising from ongoing MENCAP systems, and donations (see Figure 3.10).

The nursery team, as shown in Figure 3.11, was best described as a core (voluntary sector) and extended (NHS) team. Within the core nursery team there was a clear hierarchy with strong leadership from the nursery head in the style of a fully managed team. NHS extended team members were managed by their own line managers within the NHS. A nursery advisory group was responsible to a chief executive who in turn was responsible to a board of trustees. There appeared to be little in the way of a formal relationship between MENCAP and senior management within the NHS responsible for the NHS extended team members, but nursery staff had strong links with other agencies such as the local child development team with whom we also worked in the project.

The head injury team

National policy

Head injury is a common problem, with Department of Health statistics indicating over 100,000 admissions to hospitals in England with a primary diagnosis of head injury of which at least 30 per cent were children under 15 years (DoH 2001). Despite this high incidence of injury, death rates are low at 6–10 per 100,000 population per annum (Kay and Teasdale 2001), but morbidity after injury is high and far exceeds the capacity of UK neuro-rehabilitation services. Nearly half of those surviving after head injury may have some form of restriction to lifestyle with severity of disability not necessarily related to severity of injury (Thornhill et al. 2000).

Despite this, there is a lack of coherent policy concerning the long-term care of children with acquired brain injury in the UK, although recently a number of evidence-based guidelines have been published on managing various aspects of head injury. In 2003, the National Collaborating Centre for Acute Care was commissioned by the National Institute for Clinical Excellence (NICE) to produce an evidence-based clinical guideline on the early management of head injury in children and adults (NICE 2003). The guideline offers 'best practice for the care of all patients who present with a suspected or confirmed traumatic head injury with or without other major trauma'. Where appropriate, separate advice is offered for adults and children but the guideline does not address the rehabilitation or long-term care of patients with a head injury. A guideline published jointly by the British Society of Rehabilitation Medicine (BSRM) and the Royal College of Physicians (RCP) later in 2003 (BSRM/RCP 2003) provided complementary advice on the longer-term rehabilitation of head-injured patients. Although the advice is aimed at adult patients, much of it is relevant for the rehabilitation of children.

Prior to this, the NICE guideline reported that the first UK-wide guidelines on identifying patients who were at high risk of intracranial complications following a head injury were drawn up by a working party of neurosurgeons in 1984 and used in the UK for over 15 years with subsequent modifications published by the Society of British Neurological Surgeons in 1998 and the Royal College of Surgeons of England in 1999. In 2000, the Scottish Intercollegiate Guidelines Network (SIGN) published a guideline on the early management of head injury that included sections relevant to the care of children.

It is of note that one of the 'exemplar patient journeys' that was published to support the National Service Framework (NSF) for children, young people and maternity services and to illustrate key NSF themes concerned acquired brain injury in children (DfES/DoH 2004b).

Local practice

The head injury team worked with children and young people admitted to hospital with moderate to severe traumatic brain injury. The hospital was a regional centre and patients were admitted from a wide area. The team provided initial acute care of the child and family in the immediate aftermath of the injury. It continued to work with the family through the rehabilitation phase for months or even years in severe cases.

Most team members were based in the acute hospital. There was no formal team base as team members had offices within their own departments in the hospital. Team meetings took place in a seminar room off the ward. The main geographical focus of work was in the neurological ward itself and to a lesser extent in the hospital school, and in the outpatient clinic. This clinic was located in the same building as the child development team with which we worked in the project. All team members had other core functions but contributed some sessions to neuro-rehabilitation. At the time of the research, the team comprised a consultant paediatric neurologist and sessional contributions from a consultant psychiatrist, consultant psychologist, occupational therapists, speech and language therapists, physiotherapists, nursing staff on the paediatric neurology ward, the hospital school teacher and a social worker (see Figure 3.12).

The head injury team was best described as a network association of professionals from different backgrounds who came together because they had a common interest in coordinating the care of children with traumatic brain injury. There were no formal team/network meetings but all members met weekly as part of a larger paediatric neurology meeting that coordinated the management of all children with neurological problems in the hospital. Some internal leadership came from the consultant paediatrician but other senior team/network members also took on leadership roles for particular tasks. The team/network had regular, quarterly awaydays to discuss joint working, policies and procedures and to engage in team-building. As shown in

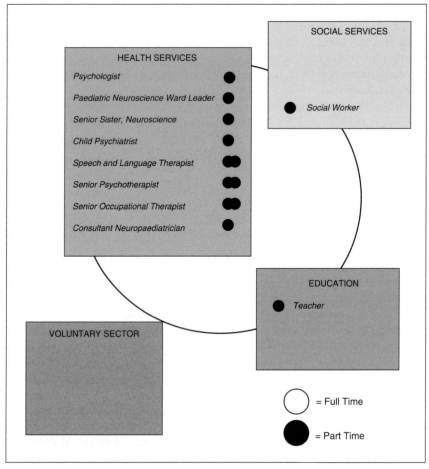

Figure 3.12 Head injury team: employment structure

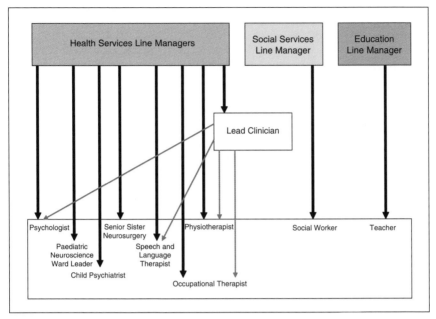

Figure 3.13   Head injury team: management structure

Figure 3.13, there were no formal links between the stakeholder agencies employing the different team/network members.

The child development team

The Sheldon Report (1968) called for child assessment teams to be set up so that disabled children could receive more coordinated services (Hall 1997). The multi-agency approach was advocated to overcome the problem of families having to tell their stories repeatedly to different professionals, and experiencing gaps in service. The Court Report (DoH 1976) endorsed the child development centre offering assessment, therapy and treatment. It introduced the concept of district teams with both a clinical and managerial function. It envisaged child development teams staffed by paediatricians, nurses, social workers, psychologists and teachers (Hall 1997). Most child development teams cater for pre-school children with cerebral palsy, severe learning disabilities and disabling communication problems such as autism and severe language impairment. There are marked variations in client groups and staffing mix in the UK, although most have been led by doctors (Bax and Whitmore 1991; Zahir and Bennet 1994).

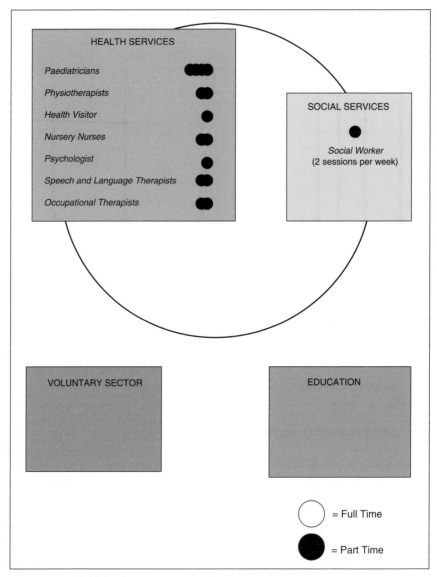

Figure 3.14 Child development team: employment structure

In 2007, the Labour Government published a crucial report with the ambitious aim of transforming the lives of disabled children. In many ways this is a typical New Labour initiative in terms of children – it is wide-ranging and ambitious, demonstrating a belief that the State can change the lives of children in a positive direction.

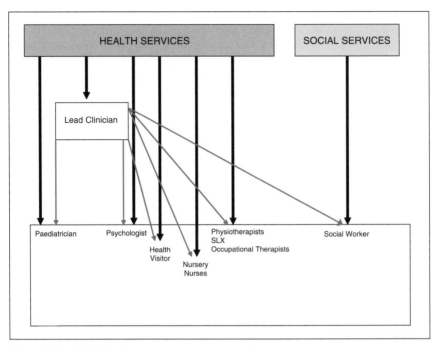

Figure 3.15   Child development team: management structure

Aiming Higher for Disabled Children argues that disabled children should be seen as 'both a local and national priority' (DCSF 2007b: 6) and the current Minister admitted that disabled children 'have not been as high on the agenda as they should have been in the past' (Balls 2007). The target was established in the 2007 Children's Plan of achieving this transformation by 2011. The *Aiming Higher* report attempts to address the needs of: 'The 570,000 disabled children in England, around 100,000 of whom have complex care needs, [who] need support from a wide range of services, and so should be benefiting even more than most from these reforms' (DCSF 2007b: 11).

The *Aiming Higher* report identifies three key areas requiring action if the outcomes for disabled children and young people are to improve:

- empowerment;
- responsive services and timely support; and
- improving quality and capacity (DCSF 2007b: 5).

Local practice

The team was set up in 1990, following national good practice guidance, as part of disability services to serve sectors of the city. For many years, practitioners were employed by the local acute NHS trust but at the time of the project most practitioners in the team were employed and managed by local primary care trusts.

The team was based in a row of converted, Victorian terraced houses adjacent to the acute hospital where paediatric services were provided. Accommodation was shared with a child protection team, a bereavement counselling service and a growth and nutrition team. The inside of the building was described by staff as a bit of a 'rabbit warren' and included narrow staircases, many small and large consulting rooms and offices at various levels, making disabled access difficult.

The centre assessed and provided services for mostly pre-school children aged 0–5. Referrals were from a wide range of sources, including GPs, health visitors, senior clinical medical officers in the community, speech and language therapists and a variety of acute hospital paediatricians. The range of disorders seen comprised: cerebral palsy; learning difficulties/developmental delay; a range of syndromes, including Down's; autism and complex communication disorders; profound multiple learning difficulties; dyspraxia; degenerative conditions; and sensory impairment. These can result in any combination of: feeding difficulties; gross motor difficulties; fine motor difficulties; delayed cognitive development; delayed/disordered speech/language development; behaviour/relationship problems; social needs; equipment/aids and adaptations needs. Weekly multi-disciplinary assessments involved all team members and the child and family. Children were offered regular ongoing input from at least two members of the team.

At the time of the research the team was funded mainly by the NHS and comprised four paediatricians, a health visitor, two nursery nurses, a psychologist, two speech and language therapists, two occupational therapists, two physiotherapists and an administrator. In addition, a social worker funded by the local authority was seconded to the team (see Figure 3.14).

The child development team was closest to Øvretveit's (1993) core and extended structure with some team members having greater time commitments to the team than others. Although the consultant paediatrician was designated team leader and had some team management/coordination responsibilities, other disciplines were line managed outside the team by their own line managers and took the lead on some areas of the team's work. The leadership style was 'hands off' and similar to a joint accountability team. As shown in Figure 3.15 there appeared to be few formal links between the different agencies that employed team members.

The challenge of managing multi-professional teamwork

All of the teams in this research had struggled with the complexities of managing staff. Agreement needed to be reached about line management responsibilities (e.g. who would authorize leave and absence), coordination of the work of the team (e.g. which team member would take on a particular piece of work), and professional supervision/support (e.g. how a particular piece of work would be delivered according to best professional practice guidelines). Because of the wide range of skills and backgrounds represented in the team, team managers and leaders often found themselves unable to provide appropriate professional support or supervision to some team members and separate arrangements were made for this to be provided by someone more appropriate. Since the passage of the Children Act, 2004, guidance has emerged for leaders in children's services – in the form of internet sources (http:// www.dcsf.gov.uk/everychildmatters/strategy/deliveringservices1/iwtraining/ training/) and training packs (Garrett and Lodge 2009).

All the teams in our sample had developed complex structures to balance the demands of different agency stakeholders and team members – although seemingly straightforward issues were often more complex when examined closely. Thus, although in some teams the three functions of line management, coordination and supervision were delivered to some staff by the same person, it was not unusual to find a team member being line managed by one person (from their host agency), coordinated by a team leader, and supervised professionally by a third person. Agencies often continued to take line management responsibility for their staff even when there was a person called a team manager. Team managers often had direct line management responsibility for some staff (delegated from stakeholder agencies) but a more coordinating role for other staff.

It appeared that many of these issues had not been determined when the teams were first formed, but had developed in an ad hoc manner over time. It is noteworthy that three of the teams seemed to have no formal reporting links with the group of agencies that funded them and therefore had limited opportunities to discuss these issues. What was clear was that only the stakeholding agencies had the authority to make final decisions in these areas. The potential for teams to be distracted from their core tasks by the time spent on resolving management structures was significant. Practical problems concerning differences in pay, leave entitlements and freedom to make decisions without referral to line managers caused real problems for team members and their managers, who reported an adverse effect on morale. Observation of team meetings and documentation suggested that other structural issues such as part-time or full-time team membership and physical location of the team (and whether all team members shared a single base) also had a significant impact on team and individual functioning.

While there is probably no one correct organizational structure for multi-professional teams (Frost 2005), it is possible to suggest some basic requirements for teams to be able to function. All team members need to be line managed and to have their work coordinated with other members of the team. All team members also need to have appropriate support for personal and professional development. Above all, team members need to have absolute clarity about who is performing each of these tasks for themselves and for their team colleagues. All agencies need to develop formal structures for liaison with other agencies responsible for a multi-agency team and to agree collectively about how the team and its members will be managed. These agencies all need clarity about the aims and objectives of the team if the team is to organize itself to deliver these objectives.

The teams themselves had developed a number of joint activities to facilitate effective multi-professional working, with considerable time and effort going into team-building and team development activities. Participation in regular team meetings was prioritized and all of the teams used occasional away days to share ideas and develop new ways of working. Team meetings and away days usually included time for collaborative reflection and active exploration of diverse perspectives, often organized around case presentation and discussion. Teams often organized shared training and/or supervision events to provide further opportunities for developing shared working practices. The creation (reification) of shared protocols for assessment and intervention in different situations was another useful focus for team discussion and for the development of a shared language and terminology for describing and discussing team activities.

More informally, participation in everyday activities such as working together to conduct shared assessments or deliver joint interventions also helped to create and maintain a sense of 'teamness', as did casual 'coffee' or 'corridor chats'. All of these activities took time and yet seemed an essential part of creating a team that could function. The stakeholder agencies that supported these teams seemed to understand this and had allowed considerable time to be invested in activities that Øvretveit described as team nurturance and maintenance and that the members of these teams often described as building mutual respect and understanding.

Conclusion

In this chapter we have outlined the way that the teams that participated in our study were organized and managed. Using Øvretveit's (1993) framework we have been able to provide a typology of team types. The national policy context and local practice of teams have been outlined and examined. We can now go on to outline and analyse the findings from our study.

Part 2
Working and learning in a multi-professional team

This part of the book explores how professionals in multi-professional teams worked together and the implications of changes in their work for their professional ideologies, identities and learning.

4 Multi-professional perspectives on childhood

Introduction

It has become common to argue that social problems and indeed childhood itself are socially constructed (Jenks 1996). The implication of social construction for our work is that the definition of the problems faced by children and their families is shaped by social forces and discourses – the problems do not exist independently of these discourses. While 'social construction' is an overarching social theory, in this chapter we are able to assess some of the minutiae of how social construction works in actual practice situations in the five teams included in the project.

Different professionals could be expected to construct 'their' service users within separate and, perhaps, competing discourses. These discourses become central to the ways professionals work together – or indeed fail to do so. We would therefore argue that these constructions are central to the joined-up agenda that we cover in this book. In this chapter we explore the many and complex issues to do with how the five multi-professional teams understood their work and defined the issues faced by children and their families.

Models of understanding utilized by professionals

In the fieldwork undertaken for the MATCh project we were able to gather a considerable amount of data relating to competing or complementary models used by professionals in the five teams. The evidence existed in relation to key issues such as assessment, defining need, predisposing factors, and current problems faced by children and their families. How did the different professionals construct and apply meaning to the situations they faced? As we have seen, Wenger (1998) argues that meaning constructed through practice is central to building communities of practice.

All the teams shared what we might call complex models of understanding:

we saw no evidence of crude, uni-causal or overdeterministic models. However, the teams had a tendency to hold a dominant model of explanation – although this dominant model was not always shared by the entire team, and was often accompanied by a secondary or complementary model of explanation.

These prevalent explanatory frameworks underlying practice for each team are shown in Table 4.1.

Table 4.1 The five team models of understanding childhood issues

Team	Dominant model	Complementary model
Young people's team	Family/systemic	Social deprivation
Child development team	Medical	Social/psychological support
Youth offending team	Social structural	Individual impact
Nursery team	Individual needs	Holistic approach
Head injury team	Medical	Social/psychological support

A systems approach

In the young people's team, the dominant approach was heavily influenced by systems theory. Throughout the period of data-gathering with this team the respondents made numerous references to how they understood the issues confronting them in terms of family functioning and systems-based approaches. The search for systemic explanations and underlying causes and meanings dominated their worldview. They believed that in order to fully understand family systems, careful assessment has to take place. A typical comment was: 'I mean, we use quite a standard assessment frame . . . where the initial assessment will go through lots of aspects of family functioning and previous history, and significant events. And I suppose we are using some kind of family assessment model really.' This was a primary method of understanding the problems the team members confronted, but it is important to note that the teams also took into account the complex 'systems' within which families are located, including key social contexts such as schools, housing and peer groups. Family issues for this team thus have to be seen as part of a 'family system' situated in a network of wider systems.

The complexity of real-life problems made it difficult for agencies to target intervention. The use of this systemic approach by a team dedicated to improving children's psychological health led the team to dilemmas of identifying boundaries between agencies. A team member reported: 'A lot of families, I think, locate the difficulties purely within the children and in fact the issues are far more systemic and that generates huge issues for all agencies because there are so many families that could fall between everybody's camp.'

The model utilized by the young people's team conceived of social disadvantage as an influence on family behaviour, but applied a 'systemic' psychological model to assessment, foregrounding intervention at the family level. There was a view that social disadvantage influenced parental competence, as expressed by the following two respondents:

> And at heart they want to get it right, they love their kids, they want to be good parents to their kids but they don't actually have a model of how you do that.

> A family is in crisis, I guess, really. Some are in crisis because of just long-term social problems; social pressures, you know, living in a very run-down area with lots of crime; lots of drug dealing; parents who've come from a very difficult background.

Thus, while wider social factors were taken into account, the practical edge of the team led to an emphasis on issues which they could clearly address through their practice. We can note therefore a potential gap between theoretical explanations (e.g. social) and the practical techniques of actual intervention. This classic gap between professional 'espoused theory' and 'theory in action' (Argyris and Schön 1976) existed to some degree in all the teams we studied.

While structural disadvantage and a resulting impact on parenting competence were important, the approach of the young people's team was qualified by the team manager and the senior practitioner who focused on social competence. Asked to describe the group she worked with, the senior practitioner said: 'I think the majority of the families that I deal with are able to access services, are able to engage in verbal therapy, are able to engage in cognitive therapy, because I think that they do have the capacity to be able to benefit from that type of treatment.' Thus the socially constructed model of understanding – that problems exist in family systems – meant that families had to be motivated in exploring these through the largely verbal methods adopted by the team.

One of the senior clinical practitioners in the team reinforced this analysis by highlighting the use of assessment and intervention approaches based on a systemic psychological model that took account of wide-ranging social influences: 'So I tend to see problems in terms of systems as being within family systems and within wider systems, meaning I'll start with the family system but then that might also include the school system, or it might include the health system or the community. But that tends to be my perspective, I'm quite systemic in the way I view things.'

The senior practitioner distinguished her approach from a typical medical model, however, because her construction of problems did not locate diagnosis and intervention in the individual: 'It really was not individual therapy. The medical model tends towards an individual diagnosis. It was very systemic.'

A medical model

In the child development team we studied, all respondents saw their practice as being based primarily on medical diagnosis. They complemented medical and practical resource interventions with the psychosocial support they offered.

A difference between this model and that used by the young people's team we have already discussed was that the starting point was the medical diagnosis of the child and/or the systems. As a result, the parents might be viewed as potential 'victims' of the actual condition and the stigmatizing tendencies in society. Like the respondents from the young people's team, the child development practitioners saw parents as the main client group. A typical comment was: 'The overall client group are really the parents and carers, caregivers, of children with developmental disorders and disabilities, but also it is the actual children, but one does work more directly with the adults involved than actually with the child.' They also expressed commitment to a model of partnership with parents:

> We're still changing partly in response to the knowledge but also partly in terms of moving further down the idea of working in genuine partnership with families which we've always thought we were doing, that kind of thing, but there's always more you can do.

> You do get involved in the emotional side of things for parents coming to terms with their child's disability or their delay; but you do the emotional as part of the practical, you know, you can go in to do a home visit to focus on something practical and spend the session sitting talking about a parent's feelings about the child and how they're adapting to the child's situation.

A similar medical/psychological model was observed in the head injury team with medical diagnosis triggering interventions responsive to the psychological consequences of traumatic injury for children and their families. As one of the therapists explained:

> Usually they have had some acquired brain injury, either from a road

traffic accident or an acute bleed or stroke as it's more familiarly known. So it's often quite, can be quite, stressful for the family and the child because obviously they were functioning 'normal' to this point and then suddenly parents and the child have had to experience intensive care.

The doctor in the team recognized the wider implications of a medical diagnosis: 'Everything from medical problems through to behavioural, cognitive, emotional, psychological, schooling, home, housing, family, family issues and problems will change depending on the age of the child.'

Respondents from a health background in this team emphasized a blend of medical intervention with psychological counselling and resource support. However, a psychologist in the team also highlighted the issues from their professional perspective: 'Stigma, impaired personal functioning, management of uncertainty, managing recovery, not just going through recovering process but managing your recovery process.' Here the same respondent reflects some of the views that we have seen are espoused in the young people's team we have already analysed: 'I think some of them are within individuals, but I think many of them are sort of, what I call systemic. Schools have to then manage a different pupil, or teach a different pupil to the one that they had previously.'

Again we noted that teams did not always share a universal worldview. The head injury team social worker claimed that consultants attached to the team followed a dominant medical model, whereas she applied a social model:

> Whereas I will get to know a family . . . I will talk to the parents, I will be able to talk to them about their other child, first name, you know 'how did he get on?', the consultants are really only interested in that child and their rehabilitation. And so what is success measured by really, is it by physical fitness, or is it about the child being able to successfully rejoin the family and the family being able to care for the child in the community or whatever? So, it depends what aspects, what models you are working with really, whether it is the medical model or the social model.

As in the young people's team, two models seem to be able to exist alongside each other – with complementary aspects – but also with some tension.

A needs-based model

In the nursery team, where all the children had special needs, there was an emphasis on the individual and unique situation faced by each child and their family: 'You see them as an individual rather than a child with special needs, so really you just deal with it as normal really, not as anything different.' Referring to her service users, another member of the team put it like this, empathizing with the perspective of the child: 'I have needs and those needs need to be met as well you know. I am a child first and foremost, but I have some individual needs.' This stress on individuality was combined with a holistic emphasis on health-related psychological and social influences on pre-school education. The importance of the family was highlighted, since the model involved parents in attending the educational setting regularly, and also involved counselling. However, the primary focus of intervention remained the individual child.

The individual needs model occurred in a context where professionals expressed fears that mainstream settings might to some degree ignore the individuality of children with special needs. A staff member viewed parents/carers as coming from different social and personal backgrounds with varying needs. This mirrored her insistence that the children were all different and they each had specific needs: 'It's trying to remember that they aren't professionals now. They're now parents. And then at the other end of the scale we've got people with learning difficulties who are now parents. And again they're going to need quite a bit of support in the home.' This model, therefore, has a strong focus on individual needs and the uniqueness of these needs – the systemic or social perspectives are relatively absent.

A social model

In the youth crime team a social model was most influential in enabling the team to understand and intervene with young offenders. When asked to define their client group, typical responses from this team were:

> If they have experienced disadvantage in any shape or form, throughout their younger life – and that could be developmentally, or financially, or physically, or emotionally – all those factors will predispose a young person to have mental health issues, or have limited resources to deal with stresses in life.

> Generally from working-class backgrounds. Nearly always poorly educated, either excluded from school or dropped out of school.

> Predominately white which is quite surprising given [where] we work ... but predominantly white, maybe 85–90 per cent white.

> I have yet to have young middle-class well-educated offenders with

'A' levels and degrees going out committing minor offences, whatever it may be, public order offences or what have you. All my client group, 95 per cent of my client group, have been, as you described, excluded, come from excluded backgrounds.

Here then, social class, exclusion and poverty predominate. However, this dominant social model contrasted with the superficially similar emphasis on social influences we have already outlined in the young people's team. In the youth crime team, influences on social exclusion were viewed as key determinants, whereas in the young people's team, social factors were seen as mediated through family systems and perceived to be key determinants of a child's emotional health.

In the youth crime team, the 'strong' version of the social model applied by the probation officer led to him asserting that psychological problems were almost not a factor at all:

But I think that's largely because 95 per cent of the people I see fit into the deprivation/economic exclusion model . . . I've had maybe one person who's got psychiatric/psychological problems since I've been here . . . the overwhelming bulk of young people we see have very, very, very similar problems; it's drug use, it's exclusion . . . there's no discussion around that.

However, these 'strong' versions of the social explanatory model existed alongside more multi-causal and complex explanatory versions within the youth crime team. The model as applied by the respondents did not imply that the children were all 'innocents'. They were seen as quite possibly 'damaged' by the impact of social disadvantage and exclusion. Here a 'pathology' model of 'damage' existed in a complex interplay with social forms of explanation.

Application of a 'strong' explanatory social model could lead to tensions. For example, one of the health-based members of the team was leading the team to increase its capacity to carry out baseline mental health assessments and conduct anger management sessions in response to a growing emphasis on mental health issues from the Youth Justice Board. This member of staff made links between this dominant model and a complementary model – where the 'social' model had 'individual' consequences.

The team manager suggested that predisposition or vulnerability to social disadvantage could occur in young people with weakened family support networks, again making links between the social model and individual impact on clients:

A lot of them don't have any parents by the virtue of the fact that they're estranged from them, or they have sort of step-parents or they've moved into care settings. And I think those kids are very, very disadvantaged . . . a very disadvantaged group and they tend to lack in schooling, lack in general ability, and they tend to be much more caught up in street culture, peer-group pressure and so on.

Strongly held views on the social explanatory model existed alongside these complex versions. However, the social model prevailed, and its practical application and explanatory relevance were exemplified by the comments of a drugs worker. For her, young people were viewed in as non-judgemental a way as possible: 'You've got to approach each individual as not one specific fault-finding exercise. There are so many things that can contribute and can build up and escalate into something that's quite devastating in this young person's life, and it's going to affect them always.' She argued that these young people's lives were in chaos due to forms of social disadvantage impacting on them, combined with their own flawed coping strategies:

It's chaotic in that there could be community issues, such as anti-social behaviour, allegations, so that's at community level, the social services' involvement . . . which may involve some form of neglect or abuse of the young person. So that would add to the chaos. And then, on top of that, you've got the escapism, which may involve using drugs or solvents or substances to try and escape their existence.

The intervention stance adopted by this practitioner was underpinned by a model in which offending was influenced by stigmatizing and disadvantageous social factors. The stance is best illustrated by the following statement: 'They don't ever come to me as a drug user, they come to me with a vulnerability to drugs issues. Because if we label them, they can become it [that label].'

Professional models of understanding

In all the five multi-professional teams we found weaker and stronger versions of the prevalent model held by different team members or utilized at different moments by the same person. We should not imagine therefore that professional identities give rise to universally fixed or shared explanatory models. The existence of internal variations in explanatory models suggests that there are dilemmas for our teams in achieving cohesion, through negotiating shared practice models, while at the same time embracing and celebrating complexity and diversity.

A challenge for all multi-professional teams is to reflect together on the models underlying their practice engagement with service users. These models are theoretical – in the sense that they are abstracted from a range of learning and experience – but they also need to 'work' in the sense that they are practical working ideologies that have to be applied in practice in everyday settings.

For all our teams, shared expertise was required to assess problems according to various criteria of complexity, in order, for example, to develop appropriate levels of intervention and to filter referrals. Part of the complexity faced by multi-professional teams was that, while they use shared expertise to assess service users on the basis of categories of complication, chronicity and severity, they were still constrained by remits, resources and prevailing models so that they were unable to deal with all facets themselves. Each team was therefore part of a web and network of resources that had a profound impact on their practice.

Conclusion

In summary, different multi-professional teams have differing modes of explanation – and these modes can exist in the same team at different times and with a differing emphasis.

What does all this mean for integrated forms of working? We regarded all the teams we explored as functioning well, as exhibiting high standards of practice and as practising to differing degrees as 'communities of practice' (Wenger 1998). Our data suggest that teams and professionals can work together, utilizing differing models of explanation. Indeed, it may well be the case that service outcomes are improved with flexible and responsive modes of explanation.

Our evidence was that 'social construction' became a reality through the workings of the teams in the MATCh project. They socially constructed the problems of the families they worked with through the exercise of a professional 'gaze'. The 'gaze' generated models of explanation that impacted on their modes of practice, treatments and interventions. Some of the policy and practice implications of this chapter will be considered in the final three chapters of this book.

Think Points

Examine the explanatory models outlined in Table 4.1.
- Do you have an explanatory model that you adhere to?
- Is there a dominant model in your work/placement setting?
- What issues/challenges arise from people holding differing explanatory models?

5 Changing roles and responsibilities in multi-professional teams

Introduction

In Chapter 3, we investigated how the organization and management of structural aspects of the five multi-professional teams impacted on the way they operated. We considered how systemic and structural aspects of teamwork constrained or facilitated individual team members in their daily work. In Chapter 4, we explored the explanatory beliefs and values that underpinned whole-team activities. We gave some examples of how dominant and subsidiary models existed side by side and showed how individual professionals worked at reconciling their own beliefs and value systems with those dominating their team culture. In this chapter we will explore how the professionals responded to changes in roles and responsibilities within team activities and what impact these changes in their working lives had on their professional identities. We regard challenges and shifts in professional identities as a central aspect of working in multi-professional teams.

Developing a sense of who we are, in particular in relation to how those around us perceive us (Harré 1983), forges our personal identities. How we are positioned within families – for example, as the 'baby' of the family or 'the pretty one' – has a huge impact on our sense of self or identity. In turn, our identity affects what we think we are able to do. It guides our orientation to the world around us and determines the kinds of choices we make about our participation in the world. For example, if a child's identity includes a belief that they are good at learning, they will persevere with activities that seem difficult, confident that they are more likely than not to find a way to do them. They are likely to enjoy and benefit from learning opportunities rather than dread them. Sometimes a traumatic event, such as a breakdown in family life, or a major health problem, will destabilize a hard-won sense of who we are. Such events may cause an individual to work towards a different identity – perhaps less sure of their capabilities, maybe more determined to overcome disabilities. So identity formation involves learning to be yourself through a complex interplay of personal histories and societal expectations. In the modern world these identities are often complex, shifting and fluid (Jenkins 2002).

So it is with professional identities. As Wenger (1998) argued, a community of practice works at two levels. At the first level, each individual member brings to the community a sense of professional identity derived from their own working history, knowledge and expertise. These individual histories and knowledge bases contribute to the potential richness and capacity of the community of practice. Identity is one of Wenger's four main organizing concepts in his model of a community of practice, alongside meaning, practice and community. As we sugested in Chapter 1 for Wenger (1998: 5), identity is changed by both personal and social experiences in the workplace.

At a second level, the community has a corporate history and culture derived from the daily working activities of the team as an entity. Members of teams are dependent on each other as they engage in activities in the workplace. Wenger wrote: 'Practice resides in a community of people and the relations of mutual engagement by which they can do whatever they do . . . Membership is a matter of mutual engagement. That is what defines a community' (1998: 74).

In this chapter we will illustrate some of the processes of changing roles and identities in integrated services for children by drawing on examples from the MATCh project. Engaging with the community of practice of a multi-professional team gives professionals new opportunities. We can create personal/professional histories of becoming someone who works in a different way and knows different things. We can learn to transform our professional identities as we take on new roles and responsibilities. However, these transformations may be painful. Our professional identities may be destabilized as we grapple with new roles and unfamiliar activities. For some professionals the pain of losing a professional identity built up over years of working in single agency contexts proves not to be worth the gain of finding a different, extended identity in a multi-professional team.

The current policy context provided by *Every Child Matters* (DfES 2003) and the Children Act (2004) has profound implications for professional identity. As British child welfare policy moves towards integration, professionals face profound shifts and challenges in terms of their sense of personal identity. These changes in their working lives, and the effects on their ability to work effectively in the new climate of inter-agency collaboration, are inevitably influenced by their personal histories, their social class and their gender. Hall (1997) has explored how these historical factors impact on the way health workers cope with the processes of multi-professional teamwork.

In Chapter 2, we described the research methods we used to explore multi-professional teams at work. At the beginning of the project we analysed documents given to us by the teams which described their aims, structures and functions. We wanted to explore the interplay between what was set down on paper and evidence of the realities of their workplace activities. So we observed and took detailed notes on what happened at two of the teams' regular meetings. We then used this evidence to ask about working realities for key members of each team at one-to-one interviews. We asked them about the interplay between the evidence we had collected regarding roles and responsibilities within their teams as defined on paper and as exemplified in their daily situated workplace activities.

The first half of the chapter will explore the insights we gained into what child-focused professionals actually do, and how this has changed: 'what I do'. The second half will explore the effect of these changes in roles and responsibilities on people's sense of professional identity: 'who I am'.

What I do

Example 1: the youth crime team

The employment and line management structures for the youth crime team were described in Chapter 3. The team consisted of social workers, a probation officer, a police officer, generic workers called youth support workers and persons nominated by the health authority and chief education officer. Their principal professional role and responsibility as a team was 'the prevention of offending by children and young people' (aged 10–17 years).

In this team, weekly team meetings were held around an oval table in the spacious team meeting room. The meetings had formal agendas and were chaired and minuted by team members. Meetings consisted of procedural/team management items, opportunities for open discussion of cases, and team professional development slots, sometimes with guest speakers. However, agenda items were often imposed by external requirements from central government or local authority edicts addressing youth crime issues.

Figure 5.1 is an example of how we recorded seating arrangements and sequences of turn-taking regarding key decision-making at team meetings.

Below is the agenda for the particular meeting we are using here as an example of the processes of the youth crime team decision-making:

- meeting calendar;
- holiday cover;
- intensive supervision and surveillance programme liaison;
- referral order developments;
- effective practice meeting notification;
- specialist information/feedback;
- training notification – mental health awareness;
- case discussion;
- administration issues.

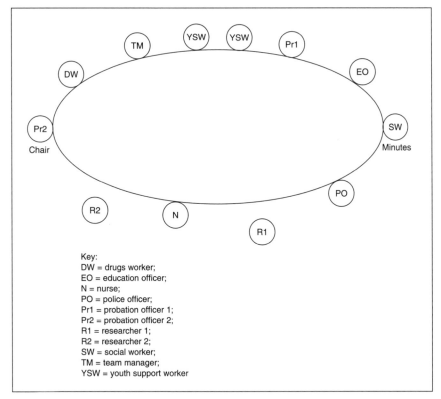

Figure 5.1 Seating plan for youth crime team meeting

We offer this example because Item 4 (referral order developments), the substantive agenda item of the meeting, illustrates a classic example of the blurring of professional roles and responsibilities in teams where workplace activities previously deemed to be the preserve of (qualified) specialists are assigned to (less qualified) generalists.

Overall in the meeting many team members contributed to the discussions during their allotted item on the agenda, and during the case discussions, though the short-term cover and agency staff said little. One of the generic youth support workers contributed substantially to discussions on pay/ responsibility issues, and on case discussion, while the other was quieter. The team manager, though not chairing the meeting, tended to lead discussions. He presented, packaged in a positive way for the context of this multi-professional team, decisions taken at local authority level in an attempt to win support for his preferred (or imposed on him by external forces) course of action.

As mentioned, referral order developments were the main agenda item.

The team manager was mediating decisions about role changes from outside the team by a citywide senior management team with overall responsibility for youth crime. The proposal was that management should transfer responsibilities for referral orders, traditionally held by specialist social workers or probation officers, to the generic youth support workers. However, the additional responsibilities were not to be recompensed by increases in pay to the youth support workers.

The team manager's preamble involved praising the team, especially the youth support workers, for doing excellent work. He explained that a local authority senior management team had decided that from now on referral orders were to be handled totally by the support workers. A new layer of external management, 'practice managers', was to be involved in supervision of the new arrangements. He assured everyone that the local authority felt confident that 'this was the right way forward'.

The team response seemed muted with a variety of low-key opinions voiced. A representative from education commented that the team could see the change as positive. A health worker asked how it would affect the support workers' current roles and responsibilities. The manager's response was that they would still do selective work on supervision orders, but their first priority would be dealing with referral orders, which they had demonstrated they could do well.

The manager asked for any further comments. After a long pause, one of the youth support workers spoke up. She raised key concerns about their pay and responsibilities. She argued that if they were starting to undertake assessment work and being asked to take total responsibility for a case, including for anything that went wrong, both these new responsibilities justified a pay increase. The manager replied that payment and conditions of service were a separate issue to be resolved in a local authority setting. He could not be responsible for this. His concern was for the distribution of work within the team, but not for individuals' pay and conditions. But he reassured the youth support worker that responsibility for referral orders overall was still to be overseen by a 'qualified' person, the practice manager, so there would be a support system for them in assuming these new responsibilities.

Teams as communities of practice (Wenger 1998) need cultural resources or 'coping strategies' to contain the tensions arising over policy-driven changes affecting working practices, roles and responsibilities. Shared cultural understandings need to be reached concerning both the purposes of change and the efforts being made within the team to ensure that professional standards are maintained while professional identities and needs are respected. The youth crime team membership represented diverse roles and professional backgrounds. As we pointed out in Chapter 3, their line management was often from outside the team. Inevitably, given their primary affiliations to mainstream outside agencies, there were differences in the way individual members were affected by proposed changes in working conditions and related pay, their roles as generalists or specialists and their own career and personal aspirations. The silences we observed were sometimes as telling as what was spoken. Often the body language of team members told us much more than their words. The relative quietness of some professionals in this episode could be viewed as strategic. No doubt they were weighing up potentially conflicting concerns. It is likely that individual professionals would be planning to advance their own interests 'off-stage', away from the public arena of the team meetings.

We were of course able to explore these conflicting views in the private spaces of the one-to-one interviews with team members when we asked them to comment on decisions we had seen made at meetings. As the interview extracts discussed below demonstrate, many of the youth crime team members did indeed have strong and conflicting views on these proposed changes in responsibilities for referral orders. A youth support worker felt that the policy change was potentially an opportunity for her to get paid for taking on new responsibilities, as reflected in the following quote: 'I think it's something we were doing anyway and we've been recognized for it. There's all the political stuff of job descriptions we're having to go into which is looking more muddy the further we go into it.' A social worker was optimistic and believed that the management had already addressed the youth support workers' concerns over pay and responsibilities: 'the management are backing them on the regrading claim and everything should be hunky-dory'. At the same time she saw difficulties in that: 'Support workers are at varying levels of ability and confidence. There's obviously going to be a changeover period.' She was also worried about the prospect of creating another layer of managers, in employing the proposed 'practice manager': 'It does leave certain questions still to be answered, yes, because the management team is still the largest in the city and it's getting larger.'

Team members who were employed by agencies and worked for the youth crime team through partnership agreements or secondment reported that they were frequently caught up in boundary disputes at local authority level about changes in professional roles and responsibilities. For example, a drug worker in the team, who regarded herself as a specialist, was asked to assume case management responsibilities. She regarded the practical problems as daunting. During her interview she told us that when she test-managed a case she 'didn't have the knowledge that was needed to address the whole thing'. Moreover, she explained to us that if she renegotiated her workload and pay for the time she spent working for youth crime teams, it would have implications for parity with other drug treatment workers working alongside her in her voluntary organization team. The impact of the complexity of the employment and management structures within the youth crime team was illustrated by the drug worker's dilemma here. She was juggling with the demands of two line managers and reflected that: 'The [youth crime] team supervision is about the individuals I am working with, and the ... [voluntary agency] supervision is about the services I am offering and the manner in which I am offering that service.'

There were further themes of loss of autonomy and threat to identity for specialists as well as the practical problems generated by changing working practices. A specialist nurse, seconded from the health sector into the team led by social services, had resisted management attempts to make her take on a generic case management role in the team. Her struggle for autonomy was related to her perception of the team culture as 'a very strong social services culture that dominates', 'for example, the belief that although I was a nurse, I should have generic responsibilities'. Extracts from her interview illustrate a robust stance when faced with the imperative to assume generalist roles and responsibilities: 'I don't do any generic work at all, and so all the work that I do is around health issues to do with young people'; 'Yes, I am a nurse, I don't write reports for court. Only stuff to do with health.'

There was antipathy to the idea that specialists within teams should not still be respected, each contributing particular strengths to the team's overall coordinated work activities. For example, a probation officer said: 'There was an idea in the probation service a few years ago, before my time, that, you know, you could do everything. That you were a mental health worker; you were a drugs worker, an alcohol worker. It's only nonsense.' A social worker also argued: 'If you're going to be involved in the life of other people, then the idea of the social worker being generic, all things to all people, should be dead in the water. Unfortunately it isn't at the moment. But certainly in our team that sort of approach has no currency.'

The youth crime team manager faced the unenviable challenge of retaining support across the team for changes imposed on him from above. Changes to one set of roles involved reshaping working practices for the entire team, and sustaining a vibrant and healthy culture, 'a culture of let's do it' and 'a heady brew' as he described it. At the same time, success in creating a new community of practice also depended on responding to the challenge of nurturing the individual professional identities of his staff. He knew that effective management was about 'the value put on people'. He believed that although the need for flexibility in changing roles and responsibilities could threaten professional identities and roles, changes also opened up for them new possibilities for learning. But he acknowledged that inevitably team members would see themselves as winners or losers. However, he was confident that the team was functioning well: 'Their cultural norms that they brought with them, have changed over a period of time. They've modified them ... and they've absorbed themselves into a multi-agency culture.'

Example 2: the young people's team

As we have seen, the young people's team was a community-based Tier 2 CAMH team managed by social services. Unlike the youth crime team, the initiative had been piloted by a group of professionals committed to changes in CAMH practices, rather than in response to a government requirement. Overall the team had far more autonomy than the youth crime team. The team employment structure was discussed in Chapter 3. Most staff members were employed by social services. A clinical psychologist and senior practitioner were employed by health. The team appointed generic child and adolescent mental health practitioners with a variety of backgrounds, for example, nursery nurses, health visitors or youth workers.

Routine team meetings were held fortnightly in a meeting room with coffee and fruit provided. A typical seating plan is shown in Figure 5.2. Though meetings were structurally similar to those of the youth justice team (procedural/team management items followed by open-ended discussion and team development work), the young people's team meetings were freer to focus on business generated from within the team priorities. Below is the agenda for the young people's team meeting:

- minutes of last meeting;
- digital camera (office thefts);
- Tier 3 pilot (Tier 2 input to new referrals management procedures);
- case file audit;

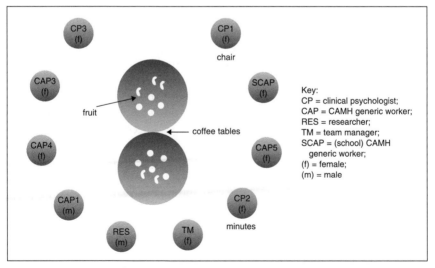

Figure 5.2   Young people's team seating plan for meeting

- CH (new person to come);
- 'best' update;
- CAMH strategy/Tier 2 development (strategy discussion);
- cognitive behavioural treatment;
- new premises;
- courses.

The manager told the researcher that hers was a 'democratic' team and this gave the team 'energy'. The meeting was characterized by episodes of vigorous negotiation and debate (e.g. concerning the new referrals procedures item) and imaginative discussions of strategic options for the future (such as CAMH strategy/Tier 2 development). Two team members carried out minute-taking and chairing duties. The manager tended to lead discussions on organizational/procedural issues, but the clinical psychologist led the discussion on CAMH strategy. In this team, contributions were more evenly spread across the team. Even so, some members remained silent for much of the meeting.

Despite their perceived autonomy, the team was also subject to imperatives from national and local authority policies. For example, an internal memorandum from the department of social services within the city council, written by the children's service manager, had been circulated to the team. A citywide 'case file audit' had been carried out during the previous month. The audit had identified that not all assessments and intervention plans were recorded on the obligatory standard file. The manager reported that more assiduous record-keeping was demanded.

The audit report also included the requirement that in 'Case closure, each closed case should be seen and signed off by the team manager.' She stressed that they had no option but to respond to this central demand, though the audit report seemed to leave some room for teams to develop their own strategies as to how they should do so. She pointed to extracts from the audit report: 'The team need to decide whose responsibility it is to outcome the referral.' 'Team standards: is an assessment required on each case? Is the intervention plan required on all cases? If not, where will the team record their plan of work?'

There was a lively discussion about how the team should respond to the citywide imperative. Different viewpoints crystallized around their shared opposition to changes imposed on the team by outsiders. The imperative for case closures to be ticked off by the manager in a centralized way was most fiercely contested. It just did not fit with their culture of 'democracy'.

Social services were 'blamed' for demanding overzealous record-keeping. It was clear that the young people's team perceived themselves as distinct from social services, with different approaches to, for example, child protection. A social services worker mentioned fear of courts as a reason for recording practices, but the psychologist argued that there was a one in a thousand chance of court procedures. Another team member said this type of record-keeping was 'foreign to the culture' of people from a health background. It was also pointed out that social services did not offer the safeguard of clinical supervision in its working practices, whereas their team did. The psychologist argued that they were 'autonomous practitioners', but that she would agree to conform to the directive by paying it 'lip-service'. The manager offered a more conformist line, stressing that the team was located within the social services structure. She conceded that the new procedure would involve her in more work, but for her it was a 'safety issue' and it 'safeguards me'. As she pointed out, 'When things go less well with a practitioner, I have to be accountable.'

The debate raged on about the relative merits of health approaches to work, where 'you don't have to do what a supervisor says', and what was perceived as the bureaucratic practices of social services where 'if it's not written down, it hasn't happened'. One of the generic workers, in fact with a social worker background, responded robustly that the children's services manager was 'treating us like babies' and 'infantilizing us'. Finally, the manager tried to resolve the argument by providing a rationale, arguing that 'to help practitioners' there is a need for 'recording'. If an issue was not written down, things could go 'pear-shaped'. It was a 'management' issue not a 'case' issue that the team needed to keep a record 'for each child'. Pragmatically, she drew the discussion to a close by asking for a group of volunteers to create their own team case file document which would enable them to comply with the citywide imperative on recording and monitoring cases. Several colleagues agreed to do so.

Resolving conflict over the external (social services) decision to impose changes in the way they kept records generated considerable 'emotional labour' for members of this team. A newly appointed practitioner sat quietly, but at a critical point of the discussion pointed out that the proposals might be a 'waste of time' regarding 'accountability', but not regarding 'quality control'. She adopted a mediating role between the strikingly opposed positions adopted by other team members. In her interview, she told us that her background as a trained psychotherapist enabled her to assess group dynamics within the team and reframe discussions to facilitate group processes and decision-making.

The very nature of their professional focus on psychotherapy and mediation made this team a particularly cohesive group. But relying on emotional bonds within the team culture could also lead to glossing over strong professional differences between practitioners. The team manager admitted in interview to the challenges of management, where both personalities and professional differences had an impact on the team's decision-making about 'what I do': 'Our styles can be quite different. We end up complementing each other but also sometimes have to think right, OK, where are each other's perspectives? And how do we dovetail them?'

Emergent themes

A number of themes about the implications of working in a multi-professional team emerged from our discussion of 'what I do':

- changes in roles and responsibilities affecting what they did were the catalyst for professionals' concern about parallel changes in their pay and conditions;
- professionals were sometimes caught up in 'boundary' disputes between agencies about what their training and background qualified/equipped them to do;
- professionals with specialist knowledge and expertise were unhappy about being 'rebranded' as generalists who could and should do everything;
- professionals were sometimes required to implement systems and procedures enforced by outsider or dominant agencies which seemed culturally unacceptable to them.

For managers, each shift in what a group of professionals were asked to do had implications for every other professional in their team.

Thus we can see that developing multi-professional teams is challenging and leads to many complex dilemmas – not all of which can be foreseen and planned for in advance.

Who I am

We turn now to evidence of changes in professionals' sense of 'who I am'. Frost (2005: 11) explores the concept of what it is to be a professional in the twenty-first century. He refers to the complex division of labour in modern society with its strata of workers based on the focus and orientation of their work; underpinning ideologies and technological/knowledge base; orientation towards clients; and status/prestige. He cites a definition of professionalism by Sims et al. (1993) as:

- a systematic body of knowledge and monopoly of powers over its applications;
- a self-regulating code of ethics, emphasizing values such as respect for the confidentiality of the client;
- the sanction of the community at large;
- control over the profession's own qualification and entry procedures;
- an altruistic orientation.

Bligh (in Petrioni 1994) described each profession behaving like a tribe, with members nurtured in distinctive ways. Professional tribes choose their own leaders and establish their own pecking orders. They impose sanctions on any member of the tribe who does not conform. They expel members who begin to demonstrate the characteristics of another tribe.

In demanding that professionals work in multi-professional teams, we are expecting them to confront, articulate and lay to one side the distinctiveness of their long-established 'tribal' beliefs and behaviours. It may seem that we are asking them to equate the high status and prestige associated with some professions working within children's services – for example, being a doctor or a speech therapist – with the lower status of others – for example, being a nursery nurse or a health visitor. These constructs of status are associated with gender stereotypes of the professionals delivering children's services – what is seen as appropriate work for men and women. In turn, the constructs have been influenced by the cultural aspirations of boys and girls implicit in their choice of careers – and on their beliefs about how much responsibility they should take and how much they deserve to be paid. Loxley (1997) points out that cultural conflict is interwoven with inter-professional collaboration because of the deep-seated social differences in the division of labour that have developed over the past 200 years in the health and welfare services in the UK.

Hudson (2002) argues that there are three potential barriers to multi-professional working:

- *professional identity:* how professionals understand themselves and their roles;
- *professional status:* how professional hierarchies and different distribution of powers are generated;
- *professional discretion and accountability:* how professionals exercise discretion on a day-to-day basis.

We were able to identify many of these conflicts, tensions and barriers underpinning the daily workplace activities of the teams and in the discourse of the professionals we interviewed. We will explore the evidence in relation to three aspects of professional identity or 'who I am' in multi-professional teamwork: what I bring from my history as a professional; who I am now; and who I am within the team.

We asked each of the professionals we interviewed to describe to us the strengths they brought to their team from the history of their previous, usually single-agency, work experiences. Typical responses were as follows:

I've done child protection work, as well as work with adults with learning difficulties and before that a long time ago – 20 years ago – I worked as a residential social worker with adolescents, and I've also worked as a community health worker.

Most of it is an education background, and then seven years of working in a child development assessment unit.

It seemed important to some interviewees who had opted to work in a multi-professional team that they had a flexible approach to work in general. For example, one interviewee explained: 'I think because I did quite a lot of agency work beforehand and I'm used to coming into teams and sort of doing my bit and then moving on and moving around, I'm quite used to it . . . I've not been like a social worker or nurse who's had a set field for so long and then have to come and redefine it.' This is significant for our study because in many ways the professionals in our teams were 'early adopters' and enthusiasts for a model which may later generate 'conscripts' rather than volunteers.

Another respondent argued that professionals need to be confident enough in their professional identity to let go of previous affiliations: 'People [in our team] don't seem to feel as though their identity is just totally wrapped up with where they've come from, with their professional background. I think that [attitude] harnesses the strengths rather than identifies the weaknesses.' It was also important for professionals that individual professional identities, related to their specialisms, were acknowledged and retained within team functions: 'we have our specialities or personal interests that we bring to the team'.

The period of transformation as newly appointed professionals settled into multi-professional teamwork could be traumatic. Sometimes their sense of who they were as professionals was destabilized. They could be distressed that others were taking on roles and responsibilities that they perceived were traditionally theirs. For example, a nurse told us 'sometimes I have to reflect on other members of the team taking on things that I might have found to be my role'. Teachers found themselves handing over aspects of their work to teaching assistants or learning mentors. Speech therapists were asked to train education staff to deliver treatments to children with language problems, now routinely integrated into mainstream schooling, for whom they would in the past have offered specialized one-to-one treatments in clinics.

One recurring concern of the professionals as they made the transition to a new professional identity was the label they were given. Their concerns were partly to do with how the label influenced perceptions of the world outside the team. As we argued earlier in this chapter, our identity is developed primarily in relation to how others perceive us. For example, one respondent said:

First of all we called ourselves project workers, which I absolutely hated, because that says we could be someone who had been employed

as a volunteer you know, off the streets, without qualifications . . .
Now we've got this new ghastly term and I can never say it without
stumbling over it and people never know what on earth that is.

Others were concerned with how the label affected the perceptions of
clients. Two examples emerged from our respondents as follows: 'I feel
unhappy with the label but I'm not sure that the community fully understands
the label. I think it can be a little confusing' and 'but most people assume
because my role is a nursery nurse that I work in a school'. Sometimes the lack
of clear labels could cause anxiety to clients receiving treatments: 'I have had
families, say, if I've done a few sessions, and they feel the problem is not going
away instantly, they will sometimes say "Perhaps we should see a proper
psychologist?" ' Here questions of status and perception emerge, indicating
that language and titles matter in the process of negotiating identity in
multi-professional teams.

Other professionals were left adrift with ambivalent labels. This is demonstrated by the following two responses: 'Well, I can't call myself a family therapist because that means something different. It's a very specific thing. I don't
know. I'm not sure. But I suppose I say I work with children and families. You
know, that's how I'd put it.' And further:

I suppose there have been a couple of incidents outside work where
people have said, 'Oh, what job are you doing now?' and I suppose
I have said health visitor because I am not quite . . . it is not clear
what. So I do feel a lack of clarity really about my professional role.
Because although I am actually a seconded health visitor, so I was very
clear about that, now that I am a mental health practitioner I am not
as clear.

Here we get a profound feel of the dilemmas posed by shifting and changing
professional identities. This is a core experience of professionals practising in
multi-professional teams.

A second concern was how colleagues within the team perceived them.
In well-established teams there was clarity that individuals were expected to
adopt a new, 'corporate' identity. So, for example, a team member told us:
'I would be worried if I heard a colleague saying "Hello, I'm a social worker in
the child development team." I would think, no you're not, you're a child
development team worker who used to be a social worker.'

In another team a professional explained that adopting a new professional
identity involved jettisoning past identities: 'I see myself, professional identity,
as a CAMH worker, that's how I see myself. I don't see myself as an ex-teacher
or a counsellor. I see myself as a CAMH worker.'

Professionals who were core to teams seemed better able to cope with identity transformations. So, for example, a core member of the child development team confidently reported: 'I think myself and the physio do a lot of role blurring together in terms of treating the child as a whole in certain aspects, but I don't feel threatened by that. I know some people probably might.' Those who worked in the team part-time or for short-term secondments, or who perhaps perceived their work to be less valued, seemed to find it harder. For example: 'You know, I have been a nurse and a health visitor for a lot of years and taught suddenly to stop being one. And there are certain situations I have been in with clients where I may be aware that the focus of my work is being driven by my background.'

There is a key issue here about differences between what we might identify as 'core' and 'peripheral' team members – an issue that we return to later.

There was also a related issue about how status affected one's professional identity. Though there was general recognition that the status of a profession had an impact on one's professional identity, a social worker reported: 'I am not overawed by working with people just because they have got a tall hat on, but a lot of people are, and I think a lot of people with tall hats are overawed by their own status as well. Sometimes people aren't listening to each other.'

More positively, there was acknowledgement that working in multi-professional teams eroded traditional constructs of power/status by demystifying what others do: 'It's broken down a few barriers, working with paediatricians. They're just like another profession to me. I don't feel the need to put them on a pedestal. They're down to earth like everyone else on the team. It's having the knowledge of the work they do and working alongside them.'

Peripheral or isolated team members had to work hard to get their voices heard. One professional said, 'Sometimes it feels undermining to say, "Well, only our way is valuable", when from my point of view I have to say, well, this is valuable and that is valuable, but sometimes it seems that is not taken on board.' Sometimes being heard was about a person's personality rather than their status or identity within a team: 'I think that because it's very rare that I have opinions, because I am usually quite quiet, but at least when I have an opinion, it is acknowledged.'

Those professionals who were able to weather the storms of identity transformation emerged with new confidence and self-awareness:

> It's made me think much, much more about the way in which I communicate my identity to others and with others. In terms of my identity, it's made me think about what I don't do and what I can't do as much as what I can do. And that's difficult because that often involves saying to people no, and that often involves saying to people yes.

Professionals, then, can emerge from challenges to their identity with a new and positive sense of their professional self.

A number of themes about the implications of working in a multi-agency team emerged for 'who I am':

- Professionals need to be confident enough about the professional identity they bring to multi-professional teams to feel safe about transforming it.
- In the period of adjusting to their new roles and assuming different identities in multi-professional teamwork, professionals may feel anxious, destabilized and vulnerable.
- Those who are peripheral to core team membership, or feel isolated as lone representatives of a profession in a team are likely to feel less well supported in transitions to new identities.
- Professionals believed that the labels assumed by or imposed on them had an impact on how they were perceived both within and outside the team.
- The perceived status of professionals in the world beyond the team did impact on team functions, but these barriers could be broken down over time.
- Professionals who struggled through the pain of transformation to the gains of a new professional identity reported an enhanced sense of 'who I am'.

Conclusion

This chapter focused on how professionals cope with changing roles and responsibilities when working in multi-professional teams and how these changes impact on their professional identities. In the next chapter we turn to the vexed question of how professionals deal with sharing their professional knowledge and transferring their skills to other team members within the daily working activities of multi-professional teamwork.

Think Points

- How would you describe your professional identity?
- Has this changed in recent years – with the development of Children's Trusts?
- If you work in a multi-disciplinary setting, is there a shared identity? Or do people hold on to their original professional identity? What impact does this have on the way you work?

6 Sharing knowledge in the multi-professional workplace

In this chapter we explore how professionals working in integrated children's services share knowledge and expertise within their teams. In other words, the focus is on 'what I know' and 'what I am able to do' in daily work-based activities as a member of a multi-professional team.

The nature of professional knowledge

There has always been a tension in the workplace in reconciling the propositional knowledge of professionals, often acquired in training for qualifications, with the application of that knowledge to the 'real world' of the workplace. Applied knowledge is initially learned as professionals work alongside experienced workers, either on placements during their initial training (e.g. nurses attached to hospital wards or teachers to schools) or in induction periods at the start of their careers (e.g. the probationary year for teachers in schools or the close supervision of therapists in their first years at work). Lave and Wenger (1991) call this apprenticeship style of work-based learning 'legitimate peripheral participation'.

Much professional knowledge remains tacit in the workplace, expressed only by implication in what professionals actually do: how a teacher structures a learning activity, how a speech therapist diagnoses speech delay, how a health visitor weighs a baby. Professionals, particularly those regarded as of lower status, have rarely been required to articulate their knowledge in action to anyone else. It may be that practitioners' only experience of explaining their working practices to an audience has been in encounters with trainees. This may have been a comfortable experience of a student 'learning by Nelly', where the trainee was in the dependent and the practitioner was in the dominant mode of learning. In contrast, in multi-professional teamwork settings, professionals are expected to explain their knowledge, and demonstrate their expertise, to a wide range of other professionals with different status, work experiences and qualifications. This may be a much less comfortable experience for a practitioner. Colleagues in teams may ask challenging questions about the assumptions underpinning their work. They really do want to understand what other team members know and do.

Eraut draws a distinction between two types of professional knowledge. He defines 'C' or codified knowledge as 'in terms of propositional knowledge, codified and stored in publications, libraries and databases and so on . . . and given foundational status by incorporation into examinations and qualifications' (1999: 3). He defines 'P' or personal knowledge 'in terms of what people bring to practical situations that enables them to think and perform. Such personal knowledge is not only acquired through the use of public knowledge, but also constructed from personal experience and reflection.'

When practitioners are asked to talk about their knowledge and skills in the workplace, they are more likely to refer to the P kind of knowledge acquired from their daily workplace experiences. They are less likely to refer to the theoretical underpinnings implicit in their activities at work. Yet this is the C kind of knowledge which formed the basis of their training to be, for example a doctor, social worker or teacher. Though practitioners rarely articulate it, they do in fact have 'theories' underpinning their practice. For example, the professionals in the five multi-professional MATCh project teams referred to theories in Chapter 4 when we discussed the constructs of childhood and treatments they espoused.

Theories are built up over years of practice as individual professionals plan strategies for treatments, encounter recurring kinds of problems, deploy particular kinds of activities and reflect on whether treatments do or do not work. Their theories are refined when familiar, expected responses from their clients do not happen. When these unexpected responses occur, professionals have to take stock, rethink their plans and try new approaches to treating clients. As they reflect on what they have learned from meeting the challenges of this particular novel case, they accommodate new insights into their ever-expanding general theories about their work. A similar process will happen following organizational or policy change when professionals confront new and initially unfamiliar problems. As we will discuss later in this chapter, this expansive learning can be strengthened when such individual insights are shared across professional teams, rather than held within just one individual professional's expanding knowledge base.

Professionals on vocational courses either at pre- or post-qualification need to be trained in both propositional (C) and experiential (P) knowledge. C knowledge is more susceptible to being assessed by written examinations and tests, while P knowledge is more likely to be assessed through competence-based models such as portfolios, observations of practitioners at work or oral examinations. These related but different forms of assessment tend to affect the status of knowledge acquired. For example, a degree assessed by written exams tends to be valued more highly than a diploma assessed by portfolios of competence. Moreover, professionals undergoing initial training tend to be trained in very specific P knowledge disciplines and related C knowledge vocational practices. This has implications for the way in which specialist knowledge and expertise are deployed, valued and paid for in the systems and structures of the workplace.

Researchers and commentators have identified the distinct agendas of professional training domains as militating against joined-up working. For example, Petrioni (1994: 84) wrote:

> The concept of inter-professional collaboration is not something that any of the professions were, or to a great extent are, trained for. Indeed they may be receiving training which specifically educates against inter-professional work. Research amongst health and social care students seems to support this view.

The policy shift towards multi-professional work has promoted a radical rethinking of the training of professionals to work in children's services, both at pre-service and in-service phases. The Children's Workforce Development Council (CWDC) is working towards a vision of the 2020 Children and Young People's Workforce. The aspiration is that the workforce should be graduate-led and qualified to a minimum of Level 3. The workforce training and qualifications initiative involves codifying the core knowledge to be acquired by all professionals involved in delivering children's services and the specialist knowledge to be acquired by, for example, play workers, health visitors or family support workers, in the form of six core competences. We will return to the broader issues of workforce reform in later chapters when we discuss the practical implications of research into joined-up thinking and working.

How knowledge and expertise are shared in multi-professional teams

Conventional models of adult and child learning emphasize the individual, private ownership of knowledge and skills. The shift towards integrated service delivery has highlighted the importance of knowledge distributed across groups of people through both formal and informal mechanisms. This concept of 'distributed knowledge' is at the heart of new ways of thinking about learning. It challenges the conventions of developmental psychology with its emphasis on the attainments of individual learners. As Puonti (2004: 44) argued: 'The human mind is distributed among people, their representations and artefacts. Knowledge, is not merely "in the head", it is also "in the world" and "between people".' Such radical new concepts demand new ways of researching them. Researchers are developing new ways of observing learning which do not rely as heavily as in the past on assessing individual's learning through language, or observing it through performances on (sometimes laboratory-based) practical tests.

Another important construct is that if knowledge is distributed across a group of workers in a multi-professional team, the knowledge will be dictated by the nature of the teamwork, its location and history. Each individual professional also brings to the team their own histories, knowledge and skills. So the combined knowledge base of teams is inevitably fluid as well as situated in a particular socio-cultural-historical context. As policy and practice shift, the knowledge base changes in response to new demands on the systems and structures of the team as an entity. But it also changes as individuals join or leave the team. In consequence, there can be no ideal model of an appropriate knowledge base for multi-professional teamwork. Rather, joined-up working can be seen as a fluctuating, local, working context and fluid set of practices where knowing and learning are characterized by tensions and conflicting beliefs.

Sorting out structural aspects of teamwork is important, but acknowledging the complexity of the processes by which the team learns new ways of working together is of equal importance. These complexities are often lost in taken-for-granted assumptions about improving the 'efficiency' of multi-professional teamwork by enforcing structural changes. Such bland assumptions do not address the 'effectiveness' of multi-professional teamwork by acknowledging the nuances of the evidence of how professionals learn to work in new ways and the centrality of informal learning. In this book we try to give equal attention to understanding and managing both the structural and process aspects of change.

Informal exchanges of knowledge

We asked members of the five multi-professional teams in the MATCh project how they shared and redistributed knowledge and expertise. They told us about the informal and formal ways this happened. The informal ways could be chats in corridors or gossiping as they stood around photocopiers: 'I think just chatting in a team room or over lunch or whatever . . . we've been very open in sharing our skills with each other anyway.'

Sometimes informal exchanges were to do with a particular client's needs. A social worker in the youth crime team explained: 'You get a young person coming through the system and you want to go and chat to someone about him or her and say "I've got this person and what do you think?" And they might know them.'

It was relatively easy to draw on the youth crime team's network of general and specific knowledge among their probation officers, learning mentors, police officers and health workers, because they all worked in the same building. In current jargon they were 'co-located' (see www.dcsf.gov.uk). Even so, part-timers who came into the team offices at certain times each week could feel peripheral to these transient networks of local knowledge passed casually between colleagues in informal exchanges.

Another important feature of the teams' informal ways of working was through social events set up with the purpose of getting to know each other and offering mutual support. Wenger argued that 'in order to be a full participant [of a community of practice] it may be just as important to know and understand the latest gossip as it is to know and understand the latest memo' (1998: 74). For teams in the MATCh project, knowledge of each other at an interpersonal level was seen to be as important as knowledge of each other as professionals in order for the team to function effectively. A member of the youth crime team explained: 'We go out maybe once every couple of months, but that's a whole team group. But in between times, like if someone's stressed or something, then we'll go to the pub for lunch.' Other teams had regular sandwich lunches together, or provided cakes to enliven team meetings on the weeks when it was someone's birthday. The interpersonal aspects of getting to know about each other established trust, so that when the going got rough in meetings, the team could fall back on relationships they had forged over time to help get through the pain of conflicts to the gain of resolutions.

Team members frequently mentioned the importance of retaining a sense of humour, particularly when stress levels were high. Typical comments were: 'We have a lot of shared humour and a lot of respect for each other and for different things, and that has been part of the success of the team'; 'Most of us have a pretty good sense of fun and I think that's important, and a lot of caring for each other'; 'I think we're quite well able to talk to each other and challenge each other and tease each other'. Humour plays an important part in helping to build and sustain the multi-professional team.

Formal exchanges of knowledge: meetings

Formal ways of exchanging knowledge were based on prearranged team meetings or training events. All the five teams valued regular team meetings as a forum for the exchange of knowledge and expertise. Some of the teams had established strategies of one kind or another to divide the business of team meetings into two halves. One half was devoted to 'business stuff', for example, reporting and disseminating information about new national or local authority policies/regulations. The other half was allocated to aspects of team functioning. For example, the young people's team 'found team meetings were becoming exhausting and we agreed, look, let's do a business part first and anything we need to reflect on and sort out and argue about is given a separate slot'. They took a break between the two halves of the agenda to share a coffee and chat informally before tackling the 'difficult' part of the meeting. The child development team arranged monthly meetings with three short meetings to discuss the pragmatics of cases and a longer one timetabled each month to focus on shared learning activities: 'So, for instance, this Friday we are looking at report-writing and in June I am doing a presentation to the team on aspects of the research I've been looking at.' Those on part-time contracts often found it difficult to attend team meetings. This increased their sense of exclusion from the processes of developing a distributed knowledge base. They could also feel dislocated from a shared understanding of agreed practices in their team.

Formal exchanges of knowledge: training/learning together

Training events could be add-ons to the team meetings. For example, the youth crime team invited experts to give presentations at their regular team meetings to update them on aspects of policy and practice where they perceived they had gaps. When team members were released to attend training events relevant to the team's functioning, they were expected to feed back what they had learned to their colleagues at the next team meeting. Other training events were one-off sessions or awaydays. Awaydays were often designed to address substantial shifts in aspects of team responsibilities and ways of working. Sometimes these expensive awaydays could be subverted into exploring ways of responding to central directives from the government. So a youth justice worker told us: 'I would like to see some time going back to team awaydays that looks at other things than just targets. Looks at relationships in the team, the fluidity, who is making decisions, who is connecting with who well, where are the developmental links that need to be worked at?'

The young people's team organized regular group supervision/seminar sessions led by different team members to disseminate their specialist knowledge and expertise among the team: 'Different people will lead depending on what we've agreed to look at. So we've looked at families that have step-parents . . . reconstituted families . . . and there's a huge amount of professional reflection and learning in those groups.'

Sometimes the training emerged from colleagues working together on joint activities. For example, in the child development team, the psychologist told us:

If you do it together, you get it together. And so actually going on home visits and doing things in people's front rooms with colleagues is what really binds the system. Because you're actually trusting each other and you're seeing each other doing it. You're not doing it separately. And you're not reading bits of paper. You actually experience the other person working with the child, or the parent, and I've got a lot out of that.

The child development team held joint assessments of the children when the whole team and the parents were present. The assessments were done by two of the professionals working with the children and parents, with the rest of the team observing through a one-way mirror. They each took turns in doing the assessments. The team used the sessions both to confer on possible diagnoses and treatments of the specific case they had observed, but also to develop a shared general knowledge base of assessing, diagnosing and deciding on treatments for their client group: 'We take turns in going to observe a child, then we give formal feedback, from what we found, to each other. And then we go back and give that feedback verbally to the parents. After that we come back together and talk about the assessment and how we have given the feedback.' This way of working requires a high degree of trust between team members. The professionals in this team told us:

We're all interdependent . . . because people all have their own roles to play and they're playing them together, that makes a team operate as a team . . . And we've got that shared role, that shared interest which is the assessment of the child and the focus on the child and family needs.

The team had experimented with videotaping some of the sessions to enable more reflection on the details of the evidence and decisions about treatments. Again such an approach presupposes a well-developed climate of trust within a team and a robust code of ethics. Research in the field shows us that the temptation with video evidence of the realities of professional practice is to focus on the minutiae of negative aspects of practice before panning back to discuss the more global, positive aspects of the events recorded. Again we noted how important humour was in coping with this degree of exposure of professional selves to others: 'We've started videoing our assessments and looking at how we do it . . . sit down and look at ourselves, and have a good laugh as well as seeing how it operates. And I think we've had the confidence to do that together, and it's been okay.'

Another kind of joint activity was when consultants observed physiotherapists and occupational therapists working together on the wards with children so that they could see for themselves what the problems might be with a particular child they were treating. When they had regular team meetings, these shared experiences and observations of the child provided 'the unified front of this is what we think' about a case. At the youth crime team, regular case discussions gave professionals the opportunity to bring different perspectives on how they might approach working with a young person 'when everything seems to be so stuck'.

Professionals also pooled their knowledge and expertise as a team to train others to work with young people. For example, 'a newer member of our team has just done a consultation with learning mentors on eating disorders, and also we did an earlier one on depression. So she has had the chance to co-teach with me, and indeed me with her, and we've learnt from each other perhaps additional skills in presenting together.' Finally, a key worker might take the role of advocate at team meetings for a particular child, pulling together information about him or her for everyone else to share. In one case the nurse at the youth crime team did an audit of the health needs of young people in general by consulting with groups of them. She then became the advocate for a client group, rather than an individual client, feeding the knowledge she had gained back to the team.

Consensus and conflict as the catalyst for learning

As we have seen, the notion of a community of practice as a place where members of the community learn from each other is a recurring theme in Wenger's model (Lave and Wenger 1991; Wenger 1998). Community members work to achieve a cultural consensus and a shared discourse about their daily work experiences. For Wenger, the association of community and practice involves three elements: joint enterprise, mutual engagement and a shared repertoire. Defining a joint enterprise is not about a 'static agreement' between members of the community, but is likely to be 'a process'. Mutual engagement brings to the members relations of mutual accountability. A shared repertoire is characterized by participation in joint activities, and their reification into objects which are external manifestations of their ways of working together. Reification might be record-keeping systems, office equipment, shared discourse and tools. Some of these reifications become 'boundary objects' designed to exemplify new ways of working at the cutting edge of emerging new practices. An example is the Common Assessment Framework to which a range of professionals and a child's parents contribute in order to focus on a case. Boundary objects can form the bridge between traditional inherited ways of working, which have been brought to the community of practice by various constituencies coming together to forge the new community.

Wenger argues that communities of practice are not necessarily harmonious and cooperative, but essentially his model is about working steadily towards agreement and stability in work-based learning. Engestrom et al. (1999: 345) take a rather different starting point. For them, interagency collaboration 'requires active construction of constantly changing combinations of people and artefacts over lengthy trajectories of time and widely distributed in space'. In the modern world of work, practice is characterized by what they call 'knotworking'. They argue that teamwork is best conceived not as focusing on particular actors. Instead it is a combination of situation-specific, object-orientated, distributed activities. As they argue, 'The unstable knot itself needs to be made the focus of analysis' (Engestrom et al. 1999: 347).

Engestrom argued that the best way to study and understand these knots is to investigate them in boundary-crossing laboratories set up in the workplace for that purpose. His techniques, involving, for example, videotaping critical incidents and replaying them to those involved, are designed to get workers to bring to the surface contradictions between their previous histories of ways of working and proposed new ways of working within their teams. Thus the recognition and articulation of conflicts are seen as an essential element in managing change. His work has been particularly focused on health settings (e.g. Engestrom 2000) where he has used videotapes of encounters between professionals and patients as the basis for dialogue about different perspectives on diagnoses and treatments.

Another important construct in Engestrom's (2001) work is that of expansive learning. He argues that learning in work organizations is too complex to be understood within standard theories of learning 'where a subject (traditionally an individual, more recently possibly an organization) acquires some identifiable knowledge or skills in such a way that a corresponding, relatively lasting change in the behaviour of the subject may be observed'. Essentially, learning is traditionally understood as a vertical process, with learners progressing upward to higher levels of competence. Instead he argues that:

> People and organisations are all the time learning something that is not stable, not even defined or understood ahead of time. In important transformations of our personal lives and organisational practices, we must learn new forms of activity which are not yet there. They are literally learned as they are being created.
>
> (2001: 137)

Engestrom argues that we need a complementary perspective on knowledge creation, premised on horizontal, expansive learning and development. He believes that both service providers and clients should be involved in cycles of reflection on evidence of real episodes in the workplace. Professionals are then prompted to use insights gained from their expansive learning to initiate new activities. In turn, reflection on these activities enables them to enter a new cycle of expanding their understanding and refining their practice.

Another important area of research and debate is how we reconcile the specialisms professionals bring to teams with the requirement for a team to operate in a holistic, general way. Atkinson et al. (2001) found that inter-agency working promotes the development of hybrid professional types, 'who have personal experience and knowledge of other agencies, including import-antly, these services' cultures, structures, discourses and priorities'. One stum-bling block is the distinct discourses or language of professionals which may exclude others from some aspects of team discussions and decision-making. But professionals can and do learn the skills of being able to communicate with each other about their specialist knowledge and skills.

Yet specialisms need to be recognized and respected within a team. It is important that they are deployed strategically for the maximum benefits of service users and most economic ways of deploying the skills of a multi-professional workforce. As the team for the ESRC Teaching and Learning Research Programme III (Warmington et al. 2004) argued, we should be able to recognize the key role of specialist knowledge within multi-professional teams, while promoting opportunities for relevant aspects of that knowledge to be distributed within the teams. Warmington et al. cite Granville and Langton as follows (2002: 24):

> There has been an ongoing tension between specialism and general-ism. They [practitioners of different disciplines] have needed to maintain and value the distinct skills and knowledge that particular disciplines offer. There is, however, an overall recognition of the con-siderable gains to be derived from the pragmatic necessity of a more integrated way of working.

If professionals feel that their distinctive knowledge base and skills remain valued while they are open to expanding their learning to enrich them, they are more likely to feel comfortable about their professional identity and gain greater job satisfaction. They can also feel reassured that their career trajectories as specialists remain intact beyond the life of the multi-disciplinary team.

Conclusion

A number of themes have emerged from the focus of this chapter on 'what I know' and 'what I am able to do' in working in multi-professional teams:

- Much knowledge in the workplace remains tacit, but professionals working in multi-agency teams are required to make it explicit for their colleagues.
- There are two types of knowledge – codified and personal – and professionals need to be trained to deploy both in the workplace.

- Professionals generate theories about their work through daily situated experiences of and reflection on delivering services.
- Multi-professional teamwork offers opportunities for professional knowledge and expertise of individuals to be distributed across the team.
- The team carries the sociocultural histories both of individual workers and of the institution, and all this changes as the nature of work and team membership fluctuates.
- Knowledge and expertise are shared in informal exchanges in the workplace and social events.
- Knowledge and expertise are shared in the formal planned contexts of meetings and training events, and in joint activities between professionals in the workplace.
- There may be a tension between the desire to reach consensus (as in a community of practice model) and to confront conflict (as in a knotworking model).
- Service providers and users can learn from each other in cycles of expansive learning to deepen their understanding of and refine workplace activities.
- It is important to respect and deploy distinctive specialisms, as well as general understanding, if professionals are to gain job satisfaction and retain opportunities for career advancement beyond the life of the multi-professional team in which they currently work.

In the last three chapters of the book we will progressively focus on lessons learned from research and scholarship for the practicalities of making multi-professional teamwork work.

Think Points

- How does learning get shared in your workplace or placement?
- Make a list of informal ways of sharing learning.
- Make a list of formal ways of sharing learning.
- Make three suggestions to improve the sharing of professional knowledge in your workplace/placement.

Part 3
Planning, implementing and supporting multi-professional teams working with children

In the final part of the book we suggest how our findings can be utilized to influence policy and practice in relation to multi-professional work with children and their families.

7 Making it work 1 – addressing key dilemmas

Introduction

In this chapter we examine two aspects of making multi-professional team-work successful. In the first part of the chapter we use the evidence we gained from discussing key incidents in the daily working lives of our sample of professionals engaged in delivering integrated services. In the second half of the chapter we extend the discussion to dilemmas common to multi-professional teams and suggest some ways they address them. The chapter enables the reader to reflect on some of the real challenges that are embedded within the integrated working agenda.

Addressing some specific incidents in multi-professional teamwork

A powerful tool for encouraging professionals to talk about their work is to encourage them to discuss specific incidents they have encountered. Discussion of specific events often leads to generalizing key principles embedded in their work. During the final phase of the project we asked members of the five MATCh teams to record in a diary over a three-month period four or five examples of critical incidents (either positive or negative) inherent in their multi-professional teamwork. We used their diary entries as the basis for designing six generalized vignettes representative of the most common types of incident they had recorded. We used the vignettes as the stimulus for focus group discussions for groups within the five teams.

Details of the vignettes are given in Chapter 2. The themes embedded in the vignettes included:

- sharing while acknowledging the importance of specialist expertise;
- using common protocols and documentation;

- excluding team members from discussions by the use of jargon;
- brokering links with external agencies;
- resolving differences in the values of team members;
- tensions arising from devolving 'specialist' activities to generalist workers.

The vignettes were generalized incidents based loosely on examples reported in the diaries. It was clear that the incidents resonated with our multi-professional teams. Several participants in the focus groups assumed that a fictionalized vignette was drawn directly from their own or a colleague's diary entries.

At the end of the project we held a validation day to disseminate to and get feedback on our findings from all those who had taken part in the project. A consensus emerged among the audience when we shared the vignettes with them. This gave us confidence to interrogate the transcripts of the focus group discussions, and notes taken at the validation day, for general themes emerging from exploration of the specific, work-based incidents and themes embedded in the vignettes.

When we explored the transcripts of conversations from each of the five focus groups, we found that the teams responded quite differently to the incidents. Teams tended to focus on either inter-personal/professional or organizational concerns. For example, the young people's team, with its history and culture of therapeutic work, discussed the incidents in the vignettes from the perspective of listening to each other's contributions. Then they formulated a sequence of problems as individuals, but from which the team gradually moved towards consensus about what they were going to do to solve the main problem. In Vignette 2.6, parents were complaining to a headteacher that learning mentors were not sufficiently trained or skilled to advise them on parenting skills. An extract from the young people's team discussion of this illustrates the process of problem formulation through dialogue towards resolution:

> *First contributor:* But it's going to become an increasing tension or dilemma when we hit an all-time recruitment crisis, you know. More and more people are moving into roles that they are not sufficiently experienced or skilled to do.
> *Second contributor:* And also certain schoolteachers being very, very dismissive about our kind of work, dismissive of certain kids.
> *Third contributor:* Or it may be that the head is right. Maybe it could be that the learning mentors should not be dealing with this level of problem, with children at risk of exclusion, and we may want to go back to the service in terms of reviewing the agreement.
> *Fourth contributor:* And not just that. You would want to know whether it was having any impact on exclusion.

A second extract from the young people's team dialogue is in response to Vignette 2.2. The incident described a paediatrician's anxieties about sharing office space and in particular the impact on the security of medical records:

> *First contributor:* Is this actually confidentiality or about the person's anxiety about their own status?
>
> *Second contributor:* You would have to be very careful not to come over as a precious practitioner who wants their own desk with their own computer.
>
> *Third contributor:* And you would have to be very clear that these were only issues that you have around confidentiality and ethics, and they were not about preciousness.
>
> *First contributor:* As you say, it needs to be clarified. What is a confidential, legal, minimal standard. And what is really about the person's status in the team.

We found that teams with a relatively autonomous approach to their work were more likely to take a problem formulation approach. Other teams with more direction from central or local government imperatives, for example, the youth crime team, were more likely to take a pragmatic, organizational line in their discussions as to how they would tackle the incidents. Their talk focused more on the systems and protocols that helped them sort out or pre-empt a problem. An example is when the youth crime team was discussing Vignette 2.3, an incident where a team member was excluding others from engaging in debates about treatments – and therefore decision-making – through inappropriate use of jargon:

> *First contributor:* I think it's really important for the management or the structure to possess a very clear remit for having that person there in the first place. Just because money's sloshing around, shall we just get this person in to do this?
>
> *Second contributor:* Could I say that one of the most important things . . . we have got rid of this myth that a case should belong to a probation officer, or a social worker and repel all boarders. In our team a case belongs to many different people. There's a lot of people involved and their knowledge and so on . . . and this person would actually be playing a real role in each case within the team.
>
> *Third contributor:* Not necessarily the specialists, but anybody who comes on board, part of their training and the getting to know the team is shadowing the other members and finding out: right, that's your niche . . . it's all part of getting to know the rest of the team members and what it is they do and don't do.

A further example of the youth crime team's orientation towards pragmatic, organizational solutions to the dilemmas is this extract from a discussion of Vignette 2.5 where a team is confronted by clashes of values among themselves and clashes over their prioritizing of parent over child perspectives in dealing with a lone parent and his 3-year-old child with complex special needs:

> *First contributor:* Eighty-six per cent of the cases we're involved in don't statutorily involve social services. But there are still parenting issues. And I think that's where our team members have achieved well. Because you have to discuss with your colleagues matters of parenting which essentially come from the different values of the team.
>
> *Second contributor:* We should have much more limited contact with parents. And there would be great use of parenting orders . . . the parent who is absent and the parent who is neglectful . . . we will be looking at much more closely in the future.

Another difference in their contributions was that the teams varied in the degree to which they were able or prepared to display dissonance to us. In general, a team was more likely to display consensus where there was a non-hierarchical management structure, as in the child development team. Perhaps this reluctance to express dissent openly was because any threat of conflict within a non-hierarchical team could potentially destabilize the hard-won dynamics of their 'democratic' way of working. Or perhaps their particular team history had promoted and achieved consensus about most treatments through previous hard-won debates long rehearsed and forgotten, and to which we had not been witnesses.

It was not just that team cultures promoted a particular approach to tackling the incidents. Individuals within teams contributed to the discussions through their own personal and professional lenses. For example, a medical worker emphasized that in contributing to team discussions about appropriate treatments, 'I would try to present some evidence base to support my view' but was later able to admit ruefully the limitations of taking a strong evidence-based approach to inform all decisions: 'Because you do get that bloody psychologist banging on about the evidence base rather than anything else they could talk about.'

Sometimes the point at which a particular professional lens would be set aside, or not, was related to the potential effect on a client. For example, a clinical psychologist argued:

> If they think we should do X and I think we should do Y, what are the consequences of doing X if I think Y is right? Are the consequences terribly adverse for doing X? And how strongly I feel about it would determine what I would do then. If I felt a real serious clinical concern

that this kid might top themselves or something terrible, I would really go for it.

The transcripts provided compelling evidence of the importance of acknowledging the socio-cultural-historical context in which each version of multi-professional practice is situated and operationalized, rather than assuming a one-size-fits-all approach to their design, implementation and management. The dialogues evidenced the fluidity and flexibility with which teams have to learn to accommodate the views of individual professionals as they come and go within the life of a team. Consequently, we would argue that managing multi-professional teams requires an approach to leadership that maintains a sense of overall direction, while being ready to adapt rapidly to changes in team membership as well as workplace priorities. To be a good manager you have to be a chameleon, responding appropriately to changing circumstances.

Dilemmas common to multi-professional teams

Reflecting on our own research and reports of others engaged in trying to understand the complexities of multi-professional teamwork, we identified recurring dilemmas confronting teams. The dilemmas operated at both team and individual levels. Sometimes individuals confronted personal/professional dilemmas that conflicted with dilemmas for the whole team. In these situations a professional had to decide whether they subjugated their personal, practical dilemmas or inner conflicts in the interest of team maintenance.

Yet we found little evidence of the recognition of the key role emotions were playing in team maintenance in either research reports or theoretical models of multi-professional teamwork. For many professionals who were catapulted into multi-professional teamwork, the emotional aspects of coping with changes in their working lives are underestimated both in the preparation and training offered to them.

The recurring dilemmas are summarized in Tables 7.1 to 7.3. We will discuss each separately before returning to a general discussion of implications of the model for implementing multi-professional teamwork. In the Appendix we provide a checklist that can be utilized by multi-professional teams in developing their teamwork.

Structural dilemmas

Structural dilemmas reported by the teams are summarized in Table 7.1. They include dilemmas for the whole team and for individuals.

Table 7.1   Structural dilemmas: coping with systems/management change

Team	Individual
Core and peripheral team membership/responsibilities/status	Full- or part-time/seconded or permanent contract and status
Line management within or without the team	Impact on shared decision-making, time, loyalties and commitment to team
Deployment of workloads/activities	Managing own workloads/time/loyalties/ responsibilities
Location of team activities	Status, access, agency within team functioning

The governments of England, Wales, Scotland and Northern Ireland are committed to mainstreaming multi-professional teamwork in delivering children's services, as outlined in The Children Act of 2004. In 2006, the Department for Education and Skills (DfES 2006) identified three models of integrated services:

- a multi-agency panel meeting around the needs of a particular case;
- a multi-agency team, often line managed by a team leader, but retaining supervision and training links with their original agencies;
- integrated services, usually co-located on one site, where permanent multi-agency teams were appointed to deliver integrated support to children and their families.

Each local authority has a Director of Children's Services heading up their Children's Trusts. Trusts are responsible for commissioning services across agencies and sectors leading to integrated service delivery. Whether initiatives are promoted at local, regional or national levels, a key finding from research and evaluations is that in order to be sustainable, they must be underpinned by systemic structural changes within the participating agencies, such as health, education, social work, employment and family support. For example, research in the USA highlighted the importance of organizational climate (the service providers' attitudes to clients nested within a cultural system) for positive service quality and outcomes for children (Glisson and Hemmelgarn 1998).

All over the UK, partnership boards were set up to oversee the management of change towards delivering integrated services (Percy-Smith 2005). The intention was that these partnerships were representative of the vested interests contributing to the work of the multi-professional team, including the private and voluntary sectors. However, partnerships, though a useful concept at an ideological level, may be too loose to be effective in practice. Long-term formal policies and budgetary decisions need to be securely established if services are to be managed and sustained effectively over time. So a key requirement for sustaining systemic, structural change is that representation on Trusts include senior officers within local or regional authorities. Without their experience, commitment and power at the macro level of local policies, complex decisions about budgets, capital investment and sustainability of services are likely to be fudged.

One aspect of the fudging of decisions is that agencies and sectors are reluctant to commit funding streams long term to the staffing of multi-professional teams brought together for short-term initiatives or flagship projects. This is a particular constraint in the current climate of economic instability. Consequently staff are often seconded from mainstream funding streams on short-term, often part-time, contracts. Being on a temporary or part-time contract has a profound impact on how committed an individual member of staff feels to their work. Often seconded or part-time staff feel peripheral to the core team structure. Whether a colleague is seconded and/or part-time may also influence the perceptions of core members of the team of their colleagues' value to the team's work.

An additional dilemma for seconded or part-time staff may be a lack of clarity about their line management. Sometimes they feel that they have divided loyalties or that their mainstream agency (which pays their salary and has responsibility for their appraisals) is pulling them in a different direction from a manager in the multi-professional team to which they have been 'loaned'. An example would be a teacher who is being asked to reconfigure services to offer informal learning through play opportunities to parents and young children attending family support services, while at the same time being actively encouraged to prepare children to acquire literacy and numeracy skills in a pre-school setting by a lead educational partner.

Managers may be uncertain about how best to deploy workloads to professionals within their teams. They have little in the way of an evidence base to help them make decisions. Though we are constantly being reassured that multi-professional teamwork is 'better' for children and their families, much of the evidence to support this claim is anecdotal. For example, it seems obvious that families with children with special needs prefer to have a key worker who collates their case history. There can be nothing more debilitating than to endlessly repeat the same information to a range of agencies contributing to their child's health and well-being. The key worker for a family may be a generic family worker.

Yet parents also need the reassurance that sustained, specialist help is deployed strategically when their child needs it. The deployment of specialist expertise and activities at point of need is a challenge for those trying to set up systems for structural change in integrated children's services. Meanwhile, professionals have reported feeling that their specialist expertise, which they know is of benefit to a generation of children, is being frittered away in endless team meetings to rethink workloads, activities and protocols to support the setting up of integrated services systems and protocols. This feeling of 'loss' may be exacerbated because often it is practitioners who have been most 'successful' in a single discipline who are seconded into radical, new ways of working in innovative multi-agency teams. They have to start all over again at rebuilding a sense of competence.

Finally, those deployed to work in multi-professional teams are often relocated to new workplaces. For all of us, the environment in which we work is crucial to our sense of well-being. Shifts in furniture, room size, workstations and rest rooms are metaphors for how much we see ourselves as valued people as well as practitioners. In a single agency setting a professional may have worked for years to 'win' a comfortable office and clinic space. For many professionals, a physical move to work in a multi-professional team may result in them losing these hard-won perks. Co-locating can be a debilitating experience. Professionals may have spent years in familiar surroundings in schools, hospitals or family centres. Suddenly their physical workplace looks and feels completely different. The mixed messages of unfamiliar configurations of furniture in integrated service settings – social services-type sofas and coffee tables, mixed with child-sized chairs for pre-school sessions and health-related consulting rooms for clinics make for uneasiness. Suddenly you do not know where you fit any more. You do not know who you are.

Yet staff told us that it makes a huge difference to a sense of belonging to a team if you are located in the same building as your colleagues. It also makes a difference if you have a workstation which you can personalize in some way. But in transferring to work in a multi-professional team base, you may be expected to work in shared spaces and even at communal workstations. Hot desking may seem to be an economic imperative to managers dealing with complex staffing and shift patterns of work, but it may not in real terms result in a more effective workforce of highly skilled and autonomous professionals.

Ideological dilemmas

Table 7.2 summarizes the dilemmas associated with ideological similarities and differences within the team.

In Chapter 4 we explored the differences and similarities in the constructs of family and childhood held by professionals with different training, values and beliefs. In turn, these constructs determined their understanding of causes and attributions of blame for their clients' situations, social conditions and decisions about preferred treatments or actions. An important example might be when a team brings their different beliefs to addressing the needs of a family where a child's behaviour is disrupting family life and impeding the child's progress at school. A social services approach might be to consider the context

Table 7.2 Ideological dilemmas: sharing and redistributing knowledge/skills/ beliefs

Team	Individual
Dominant models/disciplines/personalities	Accepting/celebrating multi-disciplinarity and diversity
Professional/socio/historical cultures colliding	Having a voice/respect for own professional knowledge and skills
Creating new forms of knowledge	Destabilization of disciplinary habits, beliefs and boundaries

in which the whole family has been destabilized. An expert on parenting programmes might argue for parallel strands of behaviour modification for both the parents and their child. An educationalist might argue for raising the child's sense of self as learner and classmate within the context of learning and socializing at school.

The important point is that these different professional voices have a right to be heard within multi-professional teamwork. In fact, the central argument for joined-up working is that the multiple perspectives enrich the treatments offered to clients. As we argued in Chapter 5, for many professionals their knowledge and beliefs have remained implicit in their daily activities and decision-making at work. Suddenly within a multi-professional team they are required to make those beliefs explicit. They are expected to articulate long-held values and defend and justify routine activities. They may only have had to do so in the past when they were involved in training students, in situations when their power was dominant. In the context of working within a multi-professional team they may have to articulate their professional knowledge and justify their professional actions to a group of challenging colleagues. This can be threatening, particularly when their status is not high, for example, when they are a 'junior' member of the team or where they are line managed by a 'high status' manager in their team from a different discipline.

In Chapter 6 we focused on the dilemmas faced by colleagues when their traditional disciplinary beliefs, habits and boundaries were destabilized. We argued that the process of destabilization can make professionals feel disempowered and deskilled. Managers need to be aware of the need to support professionals as they struggle with feelings of disorientation. It takes time for professionals to adjust to broadening their knowledge base and to learn new skills. Yet many professionals attest to the exhilaration of creating new forms of knowledge, both as individuals and within the distributed knowledge base of their teams. Sadly much of this new-found confidence and creativity can be lost as teams are broken up and displaced in response to a series of 'new' government initiatives.

An informative example is provided by the breaking up in 2005–6 of many Sure Start local programme teams, many of which were managed creatively by independent companies or charities, but which were seen to be operating somewhat erratically across the country (NESS 2005d), in order to fit them into local authority structures and systems for the launch of Children's Centres. As one manager said, 'It's like turning a huge ship around. We're like the small tug in the middle of huge waves. And I can't get my small boat on course' (NESS 2004).

Procedural dilemmas

Table 7.3 summarizes the dilemmas reported by teams in the day-to-day procedural aspects of their work.

It is one thing to think and talk about delivering children's services in multi-professional teams, but quite another to actually do so on a day-to-day basis. As previously mentioned, the model we used to try to conceptualize the complexities of the procedures of daily service delivery was Wenger's (1998) community of practice at work, in which complementary processes are *participation* (the daily, situated actions and shared experiences of members of the team working towards common goals) and *reification* (the explication of versions of knowledge into representations in the working day such as documentation, dialogue or artefacts).

For both individual professionals and teams a particular challenge is in creating the reification of common protocols, procedures and documentation. A recurring, practical problem is that many single-agency records and procedures are in a state of flux as information storage and retrieval systems are continually being redesigned to accommodate new government and man-

Table 7.3 Procedural dilemmas: participation and reification in delivering services

Team	Individual
Creating common protocols/procedures/documentation	Adjusting to other agency imperatives/issues to do with confidentiality and information-sharing
Deployment of specialists and generalists at user interface	Concerns about status/time/competence
Confronting disagreements about treatments and interventions	Holding onto/letting go of strongly held beliefs and practices
Achieving targets/goals set by local/national imperatives	Coping with pace of change/risks/uncertainties/alienation in activities

agement directives. Sometimes changes in record-keeping systems are linked to agencies being required to demonstrate that they are meeting new government targets. Databases may be completed unevenly, often because staff are not rigorously trained in how to input data correctly, in different institutional settings. Software systems may be unable to deal with an ever-increasing volume of information.

A second major dilemma is that of confidentiality. Social services staff may be concerned that confidential information, particularly in child protection cases, may be released to 'inappropriate' personnel. Medical staff are equally cautious about sharing data on individual or family health. Yet government policy, enshrined in the *Every Child Matters* agenda, is to promote the development of shared databases for all those charged with delivering children's services.

The evidence on the ground is that developing common systems and related documentation for identifying, diagnosing and delivering children's services is still a long-term goal. Some local authorities piloted information-sharing and common assessment protocols under the auspices of pathfinder projects for Children's Trusts. For example, in Bolton, a lead professional coordinates the information for children and young people with disabilities (see www.dfes.gov.uk/isa/sharing_assessment/intro.cfm). But in many localities integrated systems for the storage and retrieval of information about children and their families are still in a rudimentary stage of development.

Another major preoccupation in the workplace is how best to deploy specialists (such as midwives and social workers) and generalists (such as peer mentors for promoting breast feeding, and family support workers). In the field of medicine, where traditionally roles have been more hierarchical, systems of tiers of assessment, diagnosis and treatment have long been established. In Chapter 3 we gave an example of how this works when we described the structure of the two health-based teams in the MATCh project. But in integrated services the role of health visitors in monitoring child health may become blurred with their role in promoting better parenting. Volunteers may be trained to work alongside occupational therapists and playworkers in promoting child development. Support workers may be expected to move out of a 'comfort zone' as more activities are devolved to them and they are expected to take on more responsibility. In all this restructuring of systems and redeployment of roles and responsibilities, professionals may lose a sense of satisfaction in their job. For example, a nurse in the youth crime team resented being redefined as a 'jack of all trades'. Professionals may worry about how 'time out' on secondments from their mainstream work will affect their career trajectories. They may be concerned that they are missing crucial training to keep them up to date on professional developments within their own discipline. A speech therapist confessed that this was a real concern to her, despite acknowledging how much she had learned from her extended role in a multi-professional team.

As roles and responsibilities are realigned, questions arise as to who is competent and/or qualified to do what. Who is ultimately responsible for the quality and outcomes of services? Who takes the criticism when an inspection identifies faults in a service or when targets are not met? Is it the head of the employing agency? Or the manager of the multi-professional team to which the employees have been seconded?

Inter-professional dilemmas

Table 7.4 summarizes inter-professional dilemmas in managing the transition to multi-professional teamwork. Different pay and conditions of service are inherited from mainstream agencies. Changes in roles and responsibilities are often initiated without first clarifying how practitioners will reconcile these with their customary hours of working, holiday entitlements and pay structures. Resentments simmer as 'generic' workers perceive that there are inequities in pay, conditions and career trajectories within their teams. An example would be where teachers working in integrated daycare and pre-school education settings are on higher salaries than their managers, and yet retain their traditional 'teaching day' working hours and school holiday entitlements. In integrated services for delivering early education and childcare, local authorities are battling to formulate a common funding formula for private daycare settings, voluntary sector pre-school playgroups and maintained schools. The intention is to enable the current mixture of private, voluntary and maintained sectors to be sustainable. Workforce reform and revised pay and conditions of service will inevitably result in some providers being less viable than others. Meanwhile managers of multi-professional teams are taxed with keeping the lid on disputes over pay and conditions, negotiating with the mainstream agencies for temporary solutions to address resentments in order to maintain team functioning.

Table 7.4 Inter-professional: learning through role changes

Team	Individual
Deployments of specialists and generalists	Threats to professional identity/status and agency
Concerns about competence and supervision	'Comfort' zone and job satisfaction
Training/continuing professional development opportunities for team capacity building	Pay, conditions, career trajectories

Conclusion

In this chapter we have presented examples of the way multi-professional teams situated in different social cultural contexts and with different organizational cultures respond differently to critical incidents in the workplace. Moreover, we have argued that individual professionals within teams respond to incidents differently, each viewing the incident through a particular professional/personal lens. We argue that there is no one version of multi-professional teamwork. The teams are complex organizations demonstrating particular social-cultural-historical characteristics in particular contexts.

Nevertheless, we recognize that multi-professional teams delivering children's services in the UK (and probably wherever they are being introduced into the workplace) face common dilemmas. The dilemmas operate at whole team and individual team membership levels concurrently. We explored recurring dilemmas under four headings: structural, ideological, procedural and interpersonal. The Appendix provides teams with a tool for assessing their current stage of development and moving forward.

In Chapter 8, we move on to explore strategies for resolving dilemmas, focusing in particular on strategies for making decisions and for delivering services for children.

Think Points

Choose a scenario from Chapter 2.

- Use the scenario for discussion in a team meeting or similar setting.
- What did you learn from the discussion of this issue?

8 Making it work 2 – strategies for decision-making and service delivery

Introduction

> *There is no single way to go about integrating services for children and their families. Local conditions and opportunities for change vary so much that no-one can say, 'This is where you should start and this is where you'll end up.'*

(Miller and McNicholl 2003: 1)

In this chapter we aim to build on the previous chapter by examining the policy and service delivery issues facing multi-professional teams as they attempt to address the challenges implicit in the Children Act 2004 and its accompanying and developing guidance. Drawing on the findings outlined in Part 2 of this book we now attempt to unpick the implications of these findings for policy-making and service delivery (see also Frost 2005; Frost and Lloyd 2006; Robinson et al. 2008).

We argue that making the principles of joined-up working operate in practice involves addressing the following key themes:

- joint procedural work and inclusive planning systems;
- clear lines of accountability;
- employment conditions/individual career/role recognition;
- leadership vision;
- role clarity and a sense of purpose;
- addressing barriers related to status/hierarchies;
- agreed strategic objectives and shared core aims;
- transparent structures for communication with partner agencies;
- co-location of service deliverers;
- acknowledging peripheral team members;
- acknowledging professional diversity;
- awareness of impact of change on service users;

- joint client-focused activities;
- ongoing support for professional development;
- paying attention to 'specialist' skills retention.

Each of these themes will be examined in turn.

Joint procedural work and inclusive planning systems

Whether joint work is taking place within or between organizations, effective multi-professional teamwork requires shared procedures that have been developed with the participation of all professionals involved. These procedures become the solid representations of joined-up working, what Wenger refers to as 'reification'. However, procedures are simply pieces of paper until they are enacted through practice by the front-line professional staff. In reality, practice is an interactive process through which informed, reflective professionals interpret and enact procedures (see Bradbury et al. 2010).

We have seen exemplars in the data from the MATCh study of how multi-professional teams perform complex interactions with policies from outside and procedures from within the teams. This process takes time, especially when people from differing professional backgrounds are coming together. The development of procedures and policies requires skilful leadership from both within and outside the team.

The process of professional participation cannot be seen as static. In the real world, change occurs rapidly with new laws, regulations and changing social factors having a continuous impact on front-line practice. All of the sample teams experienced change during the 18 months of our fieldwork – including one whose role and function changed totally. This is not an unusual experience in the modern workplace (see Castells 1998). As a result of the rapid pace of change, procedures and protocols must be regularly reviewed and consulted about, and when necessary changed and reformed to reflect changes in practice. This process forms part of a learning loop where policy structures practise, but where practice should, in turn, inform and reform policy. Acknowledging the complexity of this interplay of policy and practice has informed the way we have written this book.

Clear lines of accountability

When professionals work in a traditional vertically managed environment, lines of accountability are usually clear and straightforward. When multi-professional working is developed these lines of accountability can become complex and blurred (Øvretveit 1993; and see our discussion and diagrams in

Chapter 3). For example, as we have seen, in some teams a worker might be seconded from an agency that retains responsibility for their service conditions, be line managed by the team manager of the multi-professional team and perhaps receive supervision from a third party. Joined-up, multi-professional teams therefore often have complex lines of accountability.

This inherent complexity should not be seen as a barrier to the effective functioning of multi-professional teams – but it does have to be addressed. The organization of the team and lines of accountability need to be transparent and make sense for the front-line worker. It is also important to ensure that they are offered effective support and supervision, both from within and outside the team structure.

Employment conditions, individual career and role recognition

As we discussed in Chapter 5, staff who are engaged in multi-professional teamwork will almost inevitably experience challenges to their sense of professional identity and well-being. Their sense of identity was previously built on their feelings of difference (from other professional groups) and a sense of belonging (to their specific professional group). In a multi-professional environment they are asked to reinvent themselves through a connection with other professionals. They will need time and space to reflect on their new professional identity and will require support from line managers and colleagues in dealing with the destabilization of their former professional identities.

Alongside issues of identity, there are likely to be some issues concerning service conditions that must be taken into account. Multi-professional teamwork often means different professionals doing the same work. For example, many staff are expected to utilize the Common Assessment Framework. Where professionals are on different salary scales and service conditions, they may resent this and may ask why they are not being paid as much as another profession doing the same work. Such concerns have to be shared and openly confronted. In the medium to long term, joint working seems to suggest the logic of joint national and local pay and service conditions.

As we have seen from the examples in this book, some professionals wish to hold on to their identity within a multi-professional setting. Others are willing to transform their identity within a new setting and way of working. Whichever journey staff undertake, they are likely to require support and time for reflection. It should be recalled that our sample are in some senses 'early adopters' of this new mode of working and to a certain extent are 'volunteers' and enthusiasts. As multi-professional teams have become increasingly a dominant form of organization, the staff and co-location are becoming more common, and the staff involved may be more coerced and less enthusiastic.

Further studies of the views and experiences of these staff will be required as the rollout of integrated working models continues (Atkinson et al. 2007; Robinson et al. 2008).

Leadership vision

A key variable in implementing effective practice in multi-professional team-work is the leadership offered by senior staff. In the MATCh project teams we observed highly skilled and effective leaders working on the cutting edge of practice development. Effective leadership involves individuals who can work in the ever-changing world of integrated working characterized by the skills involved in networking and boundary crossing. Such leadership has been identified in a number of studies such as those cited below:

> The most effective YOT [youth offending team] managers appear to have strong entrepreneurial skills, which they use to build good relationships with governing bodies and to broker inter-agency agreements. Effective YOTs give managers freedom and flexibility.
> (Audit Commission 2004: 57)

> We identified a number of 'boundary spanning' individuals who operated as entrepreneurs in creating new solutions to public policy problems. They had well-developed skills at mobilising political, financial and technical resources from a range of sources and bringing these to bear on particular needs and issues . . . these individuals start from the problem rather than the procedures. They are adept at managing the procedures, but only because this is necessary in order to gain access to resources that will deliver their objective.
> (Skelcher et al. 2004: 4)

Our findings also suggest that effective leadership is crucial in providing an environment that values people and celebrates the diversity of different professionals. Team members need to be encouraged to celebrate their differences, and also perceive that they are held together by a shared vision and common sense of purpose (Ancona et al. 2007).

Role clarity and a sense of purpose

One of the challenges of flexible multi-professional ways of working is that roles can become blurred and complex. This is a dynamic process of change and challenge that will have specific features in different situations and can only been fully understood in context. Effective multi-disciplinary working should not imply that people lose clarity about their roles. Just as an effective football team will contain players of different attributes and skills to create a successful team, so should a good multi-professional team. Each worker should have a clear role and a definite sense of that role and how they contribute to the overall purposes of the team.

Addressing barriers related to status/hierarchies

Exhortations to work together and to 'join up' should not wish away the reality of status and hierarchical barriers. Here we are dealing with a complex interplay of change and resistance, of difference and conflict. But when diverse professionals come together, they may well find that the differences are not as great as they imagined. Inevitably, interacting on a day-to-day basis in a co-located setting will break down some professional prejudices and ease the practicalities of communication. Equally, coming together may serve to enhance, entrench or even exaggerate aspects of difference and hierarchy among a group of professionals.

It is also the case that the dominant social divisions – around gender, sexuality, disability and ethnicity – do not magically disappear in multi-professional settings. They will remain influential forces of difference and sometimes lead to the oppression of the least powerful.

During the fieldwork for this project we found evidence to suggest that jargon could be used as an instrument of power in order to exclude staff – in team meetings, for example. Attention should be paid to the importance of clarity in the use of language and it should not be taken for granted that all members understand complex medical terms or acronyms, for example. The chair of meetings should insist that acronyms and specialist terms are explained to all team members.

Agreed strategic objectives and shared core aims

Staff in multi-professional teams need to have a clear sense of shared objectives. The success of the Youth Offending Service, for example, is largely based on their shared statutory purpose of 'reducing the level of youth offending'. They also have a shared assessment framework (ASSET) and staff members are often co-located, and they have multi-agency forms of governance. As the Audit Commission point out: 'The extent to which a YOT's governing bodies share common objectives is critical to good performance' (2004: 57).

It is important therefore that each multi-professional team has a clear sense of a 'joint enterprise', to use Wenger's phrase. The exact nature of this will be dependent on the specific setting and purpose of the team, but all teams delivering child and family services have a shared rationale within the broad framework provided by the Children Acts of 1989 and 2004, and the 'five outcomes'. The five outcomes provide a springboard for a shared sense of common purpose across children's services. The Children's Workforce Development Council have also developed a 'Common Core' of competences which can help to drive a strong sense of working together (see www. cwdcouncil.org.uk).

Transparent structures for communication with partner agencies

Most multi-professional teams have to relate to a range of agencies who may fund, second, host or manage the team. Whatever these structures and funding streams, and they are often complex, they need to be clear and transparent to providers and users of the service. For example, youth offending teams have a shared executive body on which all stakeholder bodies are represented, often chaired by the chief executive of the local authority, to ensure that partnership can be delivered from the top.

Information-sharing lies at the heart of the government view of multi-professional teams. The government clearly responded to the Laming Report (2003), finding that failure to share information contributed to the death of Victoria Climbié. This eventually led to the introduction of ContactPoint that we discuss in our final chapter. Exchange of information across agencies and disciplines is no easy matter. Different professions have different codes of confidentiality and differing attitudes towards the sharing of information. It remains to be seen how these tensions will be resolved at local, regional and national levels. Attempts so far to set up shared databases even within one agency, such as health, have been conspicuously unsuccessful.

Co-location of service deliverers

The idea of co-location is encouraged in the Green Paper, *Every Child Matters* (DfES 2003), and the subsequent stream of government guidance. The idea of co-location has become a reality in many services – with children's centres, CAMHS and YOTs providing prime examples. There is evidence to suggest that co-location (the sharing of office and other space by professionals) enhances communication, learning and understanding of roles (Frost 2005). It is important to note that co-location assists, but does not guarantee, effective joint working. Our findings indicated there can still be problems with communication and shared working activities within co-located settings.

Acknowledging peripheral team members

Our work with the teams suggests that one of the unintended consequences of developing multi-professional teams is that they can generate what we identified as 'core' and 'peripheral' team members. Core members might be those who work full-time, who are high status and to whom the team provides a major element of their daily working practice. Peripheral participants may include part-time workers, those seconded into teams for short periods, those 'hot-desking', or those who feel that they are not central to the main purpose of the joint enterprise. People can also feel peripheral where most of the team are co-located but others are not. In one extreme example from our research, a team member did not realize that she was a member of a particular team until we approached her for an interview!

Supportive and effective managers need to recognize the dangers of staff feeling peripheral and excluded, by valuing them, ensuring they have a clear and defined role to play within the team and by ensuring that effective communication channels are in place.

Acknowledging professional diversity

As we discussed in Chapters 5 and 6, multi-professional teams represent differing professions with diverse roles. While multi-professional working attempts to improve coordination between these groups, it should not attempt to ignore differences. Effective managers need to celebrate and value differences, while building a sense of collective purpose. The issue of professional identity is one of the major issues that needs to be addressed in developing multi-professional working (for further discussion, see Robinson et al. 2005).

Awareness of impact of change on service users

In this book we have focused on the inner workings of multi-professional teams. But effective integrated practice also crucially includes partnerships with service users. Practitioners should be acutely aware of the impact of joined-up practice on service users. Evidence is beginning to emerge that suggests that joined-up practice can have a positive impact on service users (see www.everychild-matters.gov.uk and *Children and Society*: Special Issue, 2009).

Joint client-focused activities

The most effective joined-up working emerges from actual practice – a strong theme of the work of Wenger. As we described in Chapter 6, the teams had a range of strategies for working together on joint activities. One of the teams worked together on real case assessments, with parents present, each contributing their own specialist knowledge and expertise. After casework they held debriefing sessions, using videotaped evidence, to reflect on how their roles and skills had been deployed. These dialogues provided powerful opportunities for developing a community of practice. Integrated practice will emerge most powerfully in actual, real-life practice settings. Active professional learning needs to be both facilitated and encouraged.

Ongoing support for professional development

Evidence from a range of sources suggests that professional members of joined-up teams experience shifts in professional identities and are constantly challenged in terms of the boundaries they work within and the changing practices they adopt. Professional skills and knowledge are exchanged and distributed among those working together. Chapter 6 described examples of professionals' informal learning at work. Informal learning happens spontaneously and can be as productive in promoting professional development as formal training, but managers need to find ways to support and enable these profound learning experiences, situated in the daily working lives of the team members.

Paying attention to 'specialist' skills retention

Workers in joined-up teams sometimes feel that their skills and expertise are undermined when there is an emphasis on team workers becoming generalists. Some felt that their professional identity would be undermined and that promotion opportunities in mainstream work could be damaged. Farmakopoulou (2002: 1052) argues that the motivation to collaborate tends to be internal to each organization. The best inter-organizational relations exist when members perceive mutual benefits from interacting with and sharing skills and knowledge with other professionals.

Conclusion

In this chapter we have made some tentative suggestions arising from implications of our work for decision-making and service delivery. In the final chapter we go on to explore the future of multi-professional work with children and young people.

Think Point

If you work in a multi-disciplinary setting, complete the checklist in the Appendix of this book (p. 132). What have you learnt from completing the checklist? What can you apply to your practice and/or your learning?

---

9 Taking multi-professional practice forward

Introduction

This book has outlined and analysed findings from the MATCh research project on multi-professional teams working with children and their families. We have drawn on the empirical findings from the project and theoretical frameworks that helped us design the study and make sense of our findings.

The aim of this final chapter is to be more speculative and to offer a contribution to the current policy debates about work with children in the context of the Children Act 2004, and its implications for policy developments. The Act provides the legal framework underpinning the implementation of *Every Child Matters*. It is commonplace to argue that *Every Child Matters* embodies the most profound policy shifts in child and family welfare and health policy since 1989, when children's services were fundamentally reformed, and even perhaps since 1948. Tony Blair, in his Foreword to *Every Child Matters* (DfES 2003) wrote:

> Responding to the inquiry headed by Lord Laming into Victoria's death, we are proposing here a range of measures to reform and improve children's care – crucially, for the first time ever requiring local authorities to bring together in one place under one person services for children, and at the same time suggesting real changes in the way those we ask to do this work carry out their tasks on our and our children's behalf.

We will use *Every Child Matters* and the official website (www.everychild matters.gov.uk) as shorthand for these profound and wide-reaching policy shifts. The website includes guidance on a range of initiatives in the field of children's services: for example, Children's Trusts and services at local authority level, Children and Young People's Plans, Extended Services and Children's Centres. The outcomes for all children central to *Every Child Matters* are broad:

being healthy; being protected from harm and neglect; being enabled to enjoy and achieve; making a positive contribution to society; and contributing to economic well-being. This is a holistic approach to modern childhood which underlines the importance of a comprehensive, integrated approach to professional intervention.

A second important Green Paper, *Youth Matters* (DfES 2005) aimed to support young people in achieving the five outcomes of *Every Child Matters*. Key principles of *Youth Matters* are: to make services more responsive to the needs of young people and their parents; to integrate services; to improve outcomes for all young people, in particular those who are deemed to be at risk; and to involve a wide range of organizations from the voluntary, community and private sectors to contribute to services. Information centres and activities are to be funded for young people. Young people are to be consulted in planning local facilities and opportunities for youth. A nominated 'lead person' in each local authority will coordinate support for young people at risk of not achieving the five outcomes.

This policy stream has been further developed by *Aiming High for Young People: A Ten Year Strategy for Positive Activities* (DCSF 2008a) which sets out 'the Government's long-term vision for improved services and opportunities for young people'.

The six key objectives established by *Aiming High* are:

1 *Rebalancing the public narrative about young people* – counteracting the unrelentingly negative perception of young people by celebrating the achievements of the majority;
2 *Empowering young people to increase their influence over the design and delivery of services for them.* When young people are involved in the design and delivery of services, they are more likely to access them and sustain their participation;
3 *Increasing the number of local places for young people to go.* Despite *Youth Matters* reforms, a lack of 'a place for young people to go' remains a concern for teenagers themselves and for parents and communities.
4 *Removing barriers and supporting young people to access local opportunities and services for them.* These may be practical barriers or personal barriers requiring intensive support.
5 *Improving the capacity and quality of services for young people.* Services for young people should be those which are known to be high quality and to have a real impact on their outcomes.
6 *Supporting and developing the youth workforce to employ the very best practice in working with young people.*

(DCSF 2008a)

The 'Youth Matters' and 'Aiming High' initiatives operate alongside an emphasis on 'Targeted Youth Support' aimed at achieving a multi-agency focus on the most vulnerable young people.

The idea of young people 'mattering' has also been used to inform the *Care Matters* process that addresses the quality of care for 'looked after' children and young people. The Green Paper, *Care Matters: Transforming the Lives of Children and Young People in Care* (DfES 2006), represents the beginnings of a major policy initiative from the Labour government. A period of consultation followed, and in the Spring of 2007, the White Paper, *Care Matters: A Time for Change* (DCSF 2007c) was published. A detailed implementation plan, *Care Matters: Time to Deliver for Children in Care* (DCSF 2008d) followed. The Children and Young Persons Act, reflecting by and large the content of the White Paper, received the Royal Assent in 2008. The reform process encourages a 'joined up' approach to children in care in order to enhance their achievement in relation to the five outcomes.

What impact can we expect of the range of initiatives – and others which cannot be covered in this context? Can we make sure that every child really does matter? Exploring relationships between the processes of public services and their products or outcomes has always bedevilled both government monitoring of the effects of changes in social policy and research into effectiveness. In 2003, a systematic review of research evidence of joint working (Cameron and Lart 2003) found 32 studies that fitted with inclusion criteria. Cameron and Lart's discussion of evidence of joint working was presented under three themes: organizational, cultural, and professional and contextual issues. Their tentative conclusion was that there was some association between the type of model of joint working and the factors promoting and obstacles hindering progress. However, they admitted that within the studies there was limited evidence on effectiveness, and that our knowledge as to what constitutes effective joint working between health and social services has hardly moved on since studies in the late 1970s and early 1980s.

A similar scepticism is demonstrated by Glisson and Hemmelgarn (1998) who undertook a rigorous, quasi-experimental study of the impact of integrated approaches on outcomes for children. These authors struggled to find positive outcomes of integrated working and they conclude that: 'Efforts to improve public children's service systems should focus on creating positive organizational climates rather than on increasing interorganizational services coordination' (1998: 401).

Despite these and other forms of tenuous research evidence of 'what works', the rollercoaster of reforms in public services charges on. Key policy messages for continuing to reform children's services are the importance of:

- a needs-led approach to the design of services at both universal and targeted levels;

- statutory inspections deploying multi-professional teams;
- better understanding of the processes of commissioning services;
- clearly designated responsibilities and accountabilities for services;
- listening and responding to the voices of children and families at local organization levels;
- better performance monitoring of outcomes and management of processes at service delivery/coordination levels;
- better leadership/management at local levels.

These key messages will permeate the discussion in this chapter. However, we will structure our discussion of how multi-professional practice will be taken forward in the UK around a diagrammatic representation of integrated services promoted by government. The diagram (see Figure 9.1) is known colloquially as 'the onion'. It is significant that outcomes for children, young people and their parents are metaphorically at the centre of the onion.

As for multi-professional teamwork, the post *Every Child Matters* agenda has shifted from a concern about how distinct agencies and professionals can contribute to integrated service delivery. Now the imperative for the joined-up agenda is to formalize integration at systemic levels nationally, regionally and locally. Integration is to be sustained at governance, strategic and operational

Figure 9.1   The 'onion' of integrated services

levels. There are four layers of the onion – governance, strategy, processes and front-line delivery – and there is a requirement to formalize infrastructures at national, regional and local levels. The key challenge is how such radical, complex and multi-level systems can maintain cohesion, information exchange and effectiveness. This is a daunting agenda for change.

Inter-agency governance

Government departments with responsibility for children's services have been reshaped into an infrastructure that leads and reflects an integrated services approach. Initially, sections from the Departments of Health and Education and Skills were drawn together into a unit responsible for services for young children. In parallel to changes out in the field, there were the inevitable turf wars as newly-emerging departments absorbed staff and settled them into new ways of working. Ten regional directors for children and learning were employed in regional government offices, linked to networks of local authorities, to support the integration of children's services across the country. Their brief was to overcome the 'bunkers' and 'silos' that constrain new ways of designing services.

Partnerships were forged at government level between health, social care and more widely, leading to interdepartmental initiatives, of which Sure Start is probably the best known exemplar.

In 2007, it was decided to follow the logic of the policy direction and form the Department for Children, Schools and Families, under the leadership of Ed Balls. This brought together the major issues facing children and young people in one powerful central government department.

One outcome of liaison and merger between the former distinct departments has been the National Service Framework (DfES/DoH 2004a). The Framework defines how services will be integrated and emphasizes the importance of outcomes. The author, Professor Al Aynsley-Green, then National Clinical Director for Children and later in 2004 appointed as the first English Children's Commissioner, argued for the principle of seeing 'the whole child' and for a shift from the concept of prevention to early intervention in promoting better outcomes for children.

In their first two terms of office, Labour policy had been to reduce the powers of local authorities. But experience of sidelining local authority infrastructures and local knowledge of systems in initiatives such as Sure Start local programmes inclined policy makers to bring local authorities back into the fold. In the end it is local authority officers who actually do the business of directing front-line managers and practitioners to deliver services. It is also local authority officers who are charged with working in partnership with the private and voluntary sectors to fulfil their statutory requirements.

Following the initial bedding in of the 2004 reforms, the government stated its intention 'to further strengthen Children's Trusts so that by 2010 there are in place consistent high quality arrangements to identify and help all children with additional needs' (DCSF 2008b).

They stated their intention to develop the role of Children's Trusts to legislate further in order to do the following:

- extend the number of Children's Trust partners;
- make the Children's Trust Board a statutory body, so that it can have specific functions;
- give the Board legal responsibility for producing and securing delivery of the Children and Young People's Plan (CYPP).

(DCSF 2008b)

Here we can see the commitment of the government to developing and strengthening the Children's Trust model – and therefore their belief that integrated working – the main topic of this book – can actually deliver improved outcomes for children and young people. The imperative for further integration and co-ordination was driven even more strongly after the tragic death of Baby Peter (Laming 2009).

National inspection of children's services

Standards of children's services are audited and measured by a complex system of statutory inspections based on the *Every Child Matters* five outcomes and led by the Office for Standards in Education (Ofsted), now rebranded as Office for Standards in Education, Children's Services and Skills. Following the Children Act 2004, all local authority services for children and young people were subjected to a joint area review (commonly referred to as a JAR). These inspections ran alongside the Audit Commission's corporate assessment of local councils. The review incorporated the inspection of youth services and replaced the previous separate inspections of local education authorities and local authority social services, as well as provision for 14–19-year-olds.

This initial system was subject to many reforms and changes between 2004 and 2008 before undergoing a major change in 2009 when the inspection regime was reformed following the Education and Inspections Act 2006. Three 'overriding duties' were established for the re-badged Ofsted:

We are to promote improvement in the public services we inspect or regulate.

We are to ensure that these services focus on the interests of the children, parents, adult learners and employers who use them.

We are to see that these services are efficient and effective.

(Ofsted 2009a)

Ofsted undertake, in partnership with the Audit Commission, a system known as the Comprehensive Area Assessment, which assesses and scores the performance of local children's services.

This process is supplemented by annual 'unannounced inspections of contact, referral and assessment arrangements for children and young people in need and children and young people who may be in need of protection' (Ofsted 2009b). This process is described as follows by Ofsted:

> The unannounced inspections are not a full inspection of safeguarding. They are an inspection of front-line practice in relation to contact, referral and assessment processes for children in need and children who may be in need of protection and an assessment of how well practice helps to manage risk of harm to children and young people and minimise the incidence of child abuse and neglect.
>
> (Ofsted 2009b)

Further inspections take place in relation to 'the joint inspection of safeguarding and looked after children within the wider Comprehensive Area Assessment' (Ofsted 2009c). The aim of these inspections, according to Ofsted, is to have 'a sharper focus on evaluating outcomes for children and young people and the impact that practice and services have on improving outcomes, including through managing risk and minimising incidence of child abuse and neglect' (Ofsted 2009c).

Here we see the heavy burden carried by local children's services. Alongside the systems we have mentioned continue the more established systems of inspections of schools, children's homes, and so on. The system presents many problems: senior managers have to place considerable energy into managing their inspection preparation and responses, arguably distracting them from supporting front-line workers; there is also a problematic relationship between inspections, measures and actual quality (see Power 1997).

Workforce reform for children's services

A second major central government initiative is the children's workforce strategy reform. A complex series of initiatives have taken place, with task groups and acronyms proliferating and changing at a dazzling rate – for example, the Modernization Agency (MA) and Development Agency (IdeA) leading to the Care Services Improvement Partnership (CSIP). More centrally to our concerns here the Children's Workforce Development Council (CWDC) was set up in

2006, chaired by Estelle Morris, former Minister of Education. It was promised £15 million in government funding for 2006–7 and £30 million for 2007–8.

The CWDC is one of five bodies which make up the Care and Development Sector Skills Council. The CWDC represents workers in early years, educational welfare, learning mentors, Connexions, foster care and social care. It also coordinates the Children's Workforce Network (CWN), made up of organizations with responsibility for teaching and other school staff, child health staff, youth workers, youth justice workers and play workers. The CWDC is charged with developing a national workforce competence framework for all those working with children; though sadly the training of teachers to work with young children remains corralled within the deeply conservative Teacher Development Agency. The aim is to review national occupational standards and the current single qualifications frameworks. As the chief executive of CWDC argued: 'People will be able to see a career path upwards as well as across into other areas as they will see how their existing skills can be built upon and developed rather than starting from scratch' (Haywood 2005: 3).

The CWDC has entered upon a large programme of work around integrated working – both assessing the extent of integrated working and suggesting models for developing and taking integrated working forward – including the 'One Children's Workforce Framework' (see www.cwdcouncil.org.uk)

The Department for Children, Schools and Families (DCSF) agenda for reforming the workforce remains a dynamic one summarized in the workforce development document *Building Brighter Futures: Next Steps for the Children's Workforce* (DCSF 2008e). This document both re-emphasises and strengthens the focus on integrated ways of working that has emerged so powerfully in this century.

There remain massive dilemmas to be addressed in reforming the workforce for children's services. For example, in the early years workforce, delivering largely care services, more than half the personnel are not qualified beyond Level 2 (the equivalent of a diploma). In contrast, in schools, 80 per cent of those working with under-5s are qualified at Level 4 (degree level) or beyond. There is a need to clarify the proliferation of qualifications in the field. We need to decide what all professionals working in children's services must know and be able to do. But we must also value specialisms and deploy specialist expertise strategically in the best interests of children and their families. So an integrated qualification framework will need to include some core requirements but some key differences. In many ways, discipline specific differences in training programmes may be more taxing to conceptualize and design than the content and processes of qualifications across the disciplines of health and education. For example, how do you delineate, codify and assess core and specialist knowledge and skills for a health visitor working alongside a midwife or a teacher working in partnership with a teaching assistant?

An extract from a report on the National Service Framework encapsulates the mood of workforce reform: 'Modernizing the way in which we meet the needs of children through changing roles and new ways of working [*involves*] the emphasis shifting from traditional professional boundaries to ensuring that the child's needs are met by someone with the right skills, whatever their job title or position in an organization' (DfES/DoH 2004a: 43).

Within the NHS a new contract for doctors and dentists has been implemented. A major programme of workforce review for other staff, 'Agenda for Change' prepared the way for a radical overhaul of working practices and pay for many NHS employees (see www.dh.gov.uk). Social work training has been fundamentally reformed to move towards a graduate and registered profession, with bursaries provided for social work students (see www.gscc.org.uk).

Workforce reform will need to be accompanied by revised agreements on salaries and conditions. We have inherited a long tradition of low paid and undervalued staff delivering children's services. The resulting structural features of such services will be hard to redress. It will require a radical rethink at a national level in terms of how an upgraded work-force will be funded.

Some progress is being made. For example, a ten-year strategy for child-care includes a transformation fund of £125 million per year to fund rising levels of pay as the qualifications and status of children's services professionals are upgraded. The new concept of 'an early years professional' has been developed in the UK. This person may be a 'new' teacher trained to work across education and care settings catering from birth to 16-year-olds, or a 'pedagogue' of graduate status trained to work across the sectors of care, learning and health. The intention was for there to be an early years professional in all the 3500 Sure Start children's centres by 2010, in every full daycare setting by 2015 and in the long term in every birth to 5 foundation stage group setting.

There has been some attempt to address inequities in the school sector. Under the auspices of *Raising Standards and Tackling the Workload* (ATL et al. 2003), classroom support workers in classrooms, nurseries and peripatetic teaching settings have been graded as teaching assistants on criteria related to the job descriptions of teaching assistant Levels 1 to 4. Levels and associated job specifications have clearly specified contractual numbers of weeks' pay. At Levels 1 and 2, staff are paid for termtime only and at 3 and 4 for 52 weeks of the year. Teaching assistants are encouraged to progress through the levels and are to be offered associated training opportunities. For example, they may study for a two-year part-time foundation degree, which will allow them access to Level 3 modules in undergraduate programmes to complete a degree programme. The foundation degree requires work placements or continuous employment so that worker competencies can be assessed by a mentor in the workplace, mostly using portfolios of evidence. Practitioners may then choose to apply for further training in postgraduate vocational qualifications, for example to train to be teachers or social workers.

Another central government strategy is to shift staff training for specialist roles into the budgets of employers. Increasingly, employers will be expected to support their staff who want to progress through various elements of training. Support may be direct, by financing additional qualifications, or indirect by offering practitioners day release to attend training programmes.

There are similar issues for workforce reform in the NHS. For example, as reforms were driven through in 2006, a major issue for CAMH teams was a new emphasis on evidence-based practice. NICE produced a number of clinical guidelines recommending evidence-based approaches to the management of problems such as depression, eating disorders and self-harm. The guidelines recommended specialist psychological interventions as being the treatments of choice; but this required a huge investment in training staff to deliver the treatments. At the time of writing this book, it is unclear where the funding for this training is to come from.

Finally, the government has recognized the complexity of managing change within the structural systems of children's services. This concern has led to the introduction a graduate status National Professional Qualification in Integrated Centre Leadership (NPQICL). The scheme was piloted at the celebrated Pen Green Centre for delivering integrated services to young children and their families (Whalley and Pen Green Centre Team 1997) and was rolled out nationwide in 2005–6. The programme, established at master's level, provides a focus on leadership for a range of professionals co-located in integrated Children's Centres, and draws on a reflective practitioner model. The programme was coordinated by the National College for School Leadership (NCSL). In the aftermath of the Baby Peter inquiry the DCSF asked the NCSL to develop a qualification for senior children's service leaders. As a result of this, in 2009, the NCSL changed its name to the National College for Leadership of Schools and Children's Services. These and many other initiatives are intended to be pivotal to training leaders and managers to achieve sustainable, systemic change in children's services.

Integrated strategy

As infrastructures for inter-agency governance are reshaped at national and local levels, a major challenge is how to reallocate resources across and within the traditional funding streams. There have been attempts to pilot the complex tasks of planning and commissioning children's services. Two examples are examined in some detail below: the Children's Fund and Children's Trusts.

Planning and commissioning services: the Children's Fund

The Children's Fund was a £920 million initiative launched in 2000 and which lasted until 2008. It was established in response to the Social Exclusion Unit's Policy Action Team (PAT 12) report on *Young People* (Home Office 2000). The aim was to develop multi-agency work for preventative services for the inclusion of children and young people aged from 5 to 13 in appropriate services in 149 local authorities in England. The guidelines for Children's Funds required local authorities to operate partnerships at both strategic and operational levels between voluntary, community and statutory sector providers of services. Guidance also required serious attention to be paid to involving children, young people and parents in the design, development and evaluation of the services.

Children's Fund partnerships were funded in three waves (in January 2001, February 2002 and December 2002). Resources went first to those areas where there was most evidence of poverty. Partnerships had to bid for money to operate Children's Funds. Once funding was ensured, they appointed programme managers and established boards to commission services according to local identified needs. Needs assessments were done in consultation with users and taking account of analyses of local community characteristics and demographics.

As with the conceptual framework of the Sure Start local programmes, the initiative was underpinned by an understanding that the identification of children or young people as 'at risk' and recognition that the causes of 'vulnerability' are complex (Edwards and Fox 2005). At-risk factors are likely to emanate from the interaction of inherited genetic dispositions of a child, family circumstances and local contexts. Vulnerability is affected by a complex interaction of these kinds of features, which shift in relevance over time. As Edwards and Fox argue: 'Such complex interactions of individual and environmental features demand equally complex responses. These include flexible forms of service provision which aim at overcoming vulnerability through multi-agency working, attention to the engaged participation of users and the building of local community capacity' (2005: 53).

The point is made elsewhere by the director of the evaluation of Children's Funds, Professor Anne Edwards, that previous versions of partnership between agencies responsible for delivering services have been led by the needs of service providers. This initiative took a radically different starting point: the changing needs and strengths of the individual client. Following the model of 'knotworking' from the work of Engestrom (Engestrom et al. 1999) referred to in Chapter 6 (see p. 84), the research methods used by the evaluation team included tracking children and young people as they experienced services. They were then able to bring professionals together to help them understand the evidence they had gathered of the users' experiences of different kinds of professional treatments and services (NECF 2004). The final report from the evaluation of the initiative, based at the Centre for Research with Children and Families at the University of Birmingham, was published in 2006 (see www.ne-cf-org). In 2008, the Fund was 'mainstreamed' with budgets and responsibilities passing to the local Children's Trusts.

Planning and commissioning services: Children's Trusts

Children's Trusts have a wider remit for bringing together all services for children and young people in an area. Thirty-five Children's Trusts pathfinders were established in 2003 to pilot the model. All local authorities were required to have Children's Trust arrangements in place by 2008, but they were encouraged to do so by 2006. Joint commissioning of services was to be underpinned by pooled resources. The expectation was that professionals would work in multi-disciplinary teams and be co-located, often in extended schools or Children's Centres.

There was no prescriptive model for a Trust, but they had to be underpinned by five principles (and here we sniff the onion model again):

- child-centred, outcome-led vision;
- integrated front-line delivery;
- integrated processes;
- integrated strategy (joint planning and commissioning);
- inter-agency governance.

Guidance notes also emphasized that unifying systems ensuring the effectiveness of the Trusts were as follows:

- leadership at every level, not just the director of children's services, but at the front line;
- performance management driving an outcomes focus at every level, from area inspections to rewards and incentives for individual staff;
- listening to the views of children and young people – on the priorities at a strategic level, and on how day-to-day practice is affecting them personally.

The University of East Anglia, in partnership with the National Children's Bureau, evaluated the 35 pathfinder Trusts and some Trusts in additional areas over a three-year period. The final report appeared in 2007 (NECTP 2007). Evaluation methods included interviews with service managers, professionals and strategic leaders; children, young people and carer/parent panels; headteacher surveys; assessment of local and national data; and cost benefit analyses

Key messages from the findings were that professionals were able to give examples in all areas of where the Trust arrangements had improved outcomes for children and families through earlier intervention and multi-professional working. Though parents were mostly satisfied with the new services, including where Sure Start local programmes had formed part of the Trust initiative, parents of children with disabilities felt under-supported. A recurring problem for these parents was access to information about what support was available to them.

Governance and management arrangements operated in some Trusts through informal 'custom and practice' arrangements, especially where there was already good practice in inter-agency cooperation to build on locally. Informal arrangements were often based on key 'hero innovator' staff. The suggestion was that in order to sustain Trust arrangements beyond the first burst of enthusiasm and commitment of these innovators, formal policies and procedures needed to be established. However, a key message was that for Trusts to work effectively, boards needed to have representation from chief executives and directors at a senior enough level to make decisions about strategic planning, management structures, budgets, allocating resources and recruiting staff.

Some local authorities were embedding Trust arrangements into their local Children and Young People Plan. The police, youth justice and general practitioners were under-represented in governance arrangements. Despite its inclusion in the Children Act 2004 statutory guidance, representation from the private sector was not included in the governance arrangements. On the other hand, where a Trust was attempting to broker multiple agreements and complicated transaction costs, the procedures for getting planning and commissioning in operation were inhibited. Some local authorities were experimenting with the pooling powers for budgets available through the Children Act 2004 legislation.

While research indicated that structural changes were in process, the findings were that at organizational levels front-line staff were still anxious about changes. Multi-agency arrangements often led to dual line management: one for work allocation within the team and the other for supervision, training and development outside the team. Trust managers needed to prepare staff for new roles and responsibilities, train them together in new ways of working and ensure that time was built into the period of transition to listen to their concerns and perspectives on the changes.

The evaluation found that accessing the views of young people and children was difficult. Professionals cited difficulties with ensuring representation and 'authentic' participation. As the summary report indicated: 'Hearing children, listening to what they say and acting on it are three different activities – this distinction needs to be recognised' (NECT 2005: 9). However, there was little evidence of parental involvement at board or at family participation levels in decision-making.

Most parents interviewed did not think that schools were suitable for co-located services such as health centres. They were worried about confidential information being held in schools. They believed this information was more secure with general practitioners and social services. They also worried that schools were already over-burdened. In relation to this finding, it is worth noting that the response rate to a survey of head teachers of 1184 schools in eight pathfinder trust areas was only 29 per cent. Only 10 per cent intended to work with local Children's Trusts. The few who were involved reported positively on the improved outcomes for children's well-being, information-sharing protocols, identification of children at risk or vulnerable, and sometimes on the specifics of truancy, exclusion and attendance.

There are emerging contradictions of policy in planning and commissioning services. For example, a government publication *Commissioning a Patient-led NHS* (DoH 2005), targeting the NHS, was brief but far-reaching in its implications. The NHS was seen as central to service delivery. Yet general practitioners were to have more say in commissioning primary care trusts. These recommendations seemed to be at odds with the rhetoric of Children's Trusts. In the end, who will control the Department of Health funding for children – general practitioner-led primary care trusts or local authority-led Children's Trusts?

There were some key lessons to be learned from the evaluations of these piloting of ways of planning and commissioning services for children at the level of an integrated strategy. It is to be hoped that central government agencies have the good sense to pause and absorb insights gained from the evaluation of pilot initiatives, before rushing into yet more strategy initiatives, spawning more government units, national working groups and assorted acronyms.

Integrated processes

A key concern for implementing integrated services is how outcomes will be monitored and measured and how information will be shared across agencies. All professionals charged with delivering integrated services must work towards the five *Every Child Matters* outcomes. It is positive that different professionals work with shared assessment procedures and protocols. However, records of children's progress kept by educational systems have emphasized individual child attainments largely in academic and some social-emotional domains. Records within the health services have prioritized developmental outcomes in physical skills and language development, as well as information about illnesses, hospitalization or chronic conditions such as asthma or attention deficit disorder. Records within children's social care have focused on family functioning and individual child case histories. How will these disparate priorities be reconciled in shared assessment protocols and tools?

A further concern is that where information is shared across agencies, confidentiality will be threatened. We have already seen how parents have expressed anxiety about the confidentiality of records of their families where services are integrated and co-located. Furthermore, even within distinct agency information storage systems at national and local levels, there has been chaos reported in attempts to set up efficient databases. For example, an article in the *Guardian* in January 2006 (Cross 2006) reported that a much heralded consumer choice information technology system enabling NHS patients to 'choose and book' treatments had been interrupted as it was launched! There were problems with the underlying digital 'spine' designed to connect all parts of the NHS in England. The spine was designed to control access to NHS systems as well as providing basic 'demographic' data about patients – names, health service identity numbers, addresses and dates of birth. This failure does not bode well for other government information technology schemes for public services. How are we to manage sharing information across agencies when current systems in place within agencies are proving to be dysfunctional?

The Common Assessment Framework (CAF)

The Common Assessment Framework (CAF) was piloted in 2005–6 in 12 areas across England, and since then has been a mainstay of the *Every Child Matters* approach. The Framework is a standardized approach to assessing children's needs for services. It can be used on its own or in conjunction with specialist or universal assessments. It consists of:

- a pre-assessment checklist to identify children who would benefit from a CAF;
- a process of gathering information on a child to identify their strengths and needs, based on discussions with the child, parents/ carers and a range of professionals;
- a standard form for recording and, where appropriate, sharing information about the assessment and reducing duplication across agencies.

There is a government website (www.dfes.gov/ISA/sharing_Assessment/ caf.cfm) listing implementation guidance and training materials related to the CAF initiative.

In the UK health sector a National Health Care Record initiative, *Connecting for Health*, is to be developed. The brief is to design a system of allowing agencies access to information about children while maintaining confidentiality of sensitive material. It is allegedly to be the largest civilian information technology project in the world.

Information sharing

At the time of writing, the aims of government policy on information sharing were that all children would get access to the universal education and health services to which they were entitled, and that children and young people with additional needs would get the right targeted services at the right time. Information sharing would require professionals to work across traditional boundaries and learn to communicate effectively with each other in the best interests of service users.

In 2005, the Children's Rights Alliance for England produced a 70-page draft guidance pack for consultation for the government to guide adults working with children to improve their lives, protecting them from mistreatment and preventing them from committing crime. The guidance included advice on how information should be shared, how to gain informed consent from children, young people, parents and guardians, and rules and laws about information sharing. The guidance was accompanied by training packs and DVDs, called *Ready, Steady, Change*, for professionals, showing how to work with both adults and young people in encouraging them to participate in information sharing (see www.crae.org.uk for more information).

The detailed way in which outcomes for most children were to be measured and recorded are likely to vary according to local authorities' contexts and current protocols and procedures. It is hoped that professionals will build on their current effective assessment and record-keeping systems. For example, daycare and pre-school settings tend to keep detailed and extensive records of children's progression, and to share them regularly with parents/ carers. However, daycare settings, often catering for children under 3, tend to prioritize in their records children's progression in physical and social-emotional domains, as well as records of their daily eating, resting and toileting routines. Pre-schools tend to record attainments in the Foundation Stage areas of experience (cited in Chapter 1). Now there is an expectation of common features of assessment across all agencies. For example, the likely indicators for progress for children under 5 with reference to the five *Every Child Matters* outcomes are currently:

- health, such as height and weight, normal language development;
- safety, such as percentage of local accident and emergency attendances for young children;
- enjoyment, such as universal access to play-based experiences;
- achievement, such as progress through the Foundation Stage profile;

- contribution, such as how integrated the families are into local community networks and services;
- economic well-being, such as the number of young children in households where at least one parent is working.

For many single agencies these are unfamiliar measures of progression to be included in monitoring and recording the development of a child. It will be a huge challenge at local and national levels to overcome the professional, ethical and technical obstacles to achieving common assessment and information sharing in multi-professional teams.

ContactPoint is an example of information sharing and perhaps forms the most controversial element of the *Every Child Matters* approach. *ContactPoint* is a computer-based database that holds the following information on every young person in England:

- Name, address, gender, date of birth and an identifying number for all children in England (up to their 18th birthday).
- Name and contact details for:
  - parents or carers
  - educational setting (e.g. school)
  - primary medical practitioner (e.g. GP practice)
  - other services working with the child.
- Indicator to show if a practitioner is the lead professional for a child and/or if they have completed an assessment under the Common Assessment Framework (CAF).

ContactPoint raises many of the generic concerns – connected with privacy and accuracy for example – that citizens have about data being held on them. It is perhaps the only aspect of the *Every Child Matters* programme which has been opposed by significant group of stakeholders (see Garrett 2005).

Integrated front-line delivery

Probably the most extensive evidence base we have so far of a model of front-line delivery of integrated services, involving co-location and multidisciplinary delivery of services, is from the National Evaluation of Sure Start (NESS) local programmes. The six-year evaluation was based at the Institute for the Study of Children, Families and Social Issues at Birkbeck College, London. It reported finally in 2006 (see www.ness.bbk.ac.uk).

As described in Chapter 1, 524 Sure Start local programmes (SSLPs) were set up in the most disadvantaged areas of England to address the government's policy of reducing child poverty and social exclusion. The target was families with children aged under 4 within a 3-mile radius in areas demonstrating high levels of social exclusion. The intervention was designed to address targets for improvements in health, education, social welfare, family support and employability. The whole community within the area was the target for enhanced outcomes. It was a radical and courageous attempt to lift the most deprived families in the country out of cycles of underachievement, poor health, limited employment opportunities and low aspirations.

The underpinning theoretical model for the intervention was an eco-logical model of child development (Bronfenbrenner 1979). Bronfenbrenner's seminal model argued that too little attention had been paid in theories of child development to 'the person's behaviour in more than one setting' or 'the way in which relations between settings can affect what happens within them'. He argued for the importance of 'the recognition that environmental events and conditions outside any immediate setting containing the person can have a profound influence on behaviour and development within that setting' (1979: 18). He also argued that the developing person is an active agent in the environment, 'a growing dynamic entity that progressively moves into and restructures the milieu in which it resides' (p. 21). He believed that 'the interaction between a person and an environment is viewed as two-dimensional, that is characterised by reciprocity' (p. 22).

His model defines a complex hierarchy of systems in which individual actions between people are nested. The systems are at micro (the immediate settings in which a child may be at any one time), meso (networks or relation-ships of settings a child inhabits), exo (settings where the child is not an active agent but in which events occur that affect or are affected by what happens in micro and meso systems) and macro levels (historical/social/cultural/ecological environments at national policy level).

The NESS evaluation model reflected the importance of acknowledging the interrelated nature of influences on child and family well-being and development. The evaluation had the interrelated strands of impact, imple-mentation, local context analysis and cost benefit analysis, as well as a module supporting local evaluations. The evaluation focused on the first four rounds of the Sure Start local programmes, 260 programmes in all. Key messages from reports (see www.ness.bbk.ac.uk) were that there is a small but significant effect of the multi-level intervention on improvements in some aspects of parenting, but less evidence of impact on the children in the Sure Start com-munities (NESS 2005a). In the early findings where there were indications of enhanced outcomes for families, they tended to be found in the 'better-off' families in the communities, and not among teenage mothers, lone parents or workless households – the very families the intervention was designed to target. Later findings (NESS 2008) indicated that these between family/demographic differences were not in evidence. It seemed that programmes had extended their interventions to a broader range of family types, drawing in those categorized as 'hard to reach', so that by 2008, SSLP effects appeared generalizable across population sub-groups in SSLP areas (e.g workless households and teen mothers).

Implementation of this complex initiative was much slower than expected and inter-agency and multi-professional working was very challenging. The implementation of joined-up services at the front line was influenced by the following tensions:

- selectivity versus universality;
- locally expressed need versus central government-determined need;
- the needs and rights of children versus those of their parents;
- evidence-based rather than entitlement-based services.

(NESS 2005b)

However, the findings were that some Sure Start local programmes were more effective than others in their impact on child and parent outcomes (NESS 2005c). The team designed a tool for rating, on a seven-point scale, 18 dimensions of programme implementation. The dimensions related to which services were implemented (service quantity, service delivery, identification of users, reach, strategies for improving reach, service innovation and flexibility); the processes underpinning the proficiency of which services were delivered (partnership composition and functioning, leadership/management, multi-agency working, access to services, use of evaluation and staff turnover); and holistic aspects of service implementation (vision, communications, empowerment of professionals and users, and ethos). In addition, information was collated and analysed on inherited, improved and new services related to child, parent, family and community needs and on the staffing of services (proportions of staff involved in outreach, family support, play and childcare or health-related activities). Findings indicated a degree of linkage between the process by which the programmes were implemented and the products of child and parenting outcomes. However, multi-agency working did not appear to be a particularly significant dimension of effectiveness.

By 2008, the NESS evaluation reported a variety of beneficial effects for children and their families, living in SSLP areas, when children were 3 years old. SSLP area children showed better social development and exhibited more positive social behaviour and greater independence/self-regulation that non-SSLP counterparts. Parents showed less negative parenting behaviours and provided their children with a better home learning environment.

Evidence from the emerging evaluation of the Sure Start programmes was influential in determining the content of the Sure Start Children's Centre practice guidance (www.dcsf.gov.uk). The guidance specifies three broad levels of services to be delivered by Children's Centres according to family needs:

- core entitlements for all families with children aged under 5, comprising information on children's services and employment/training and childcare and parenting support, pre-school provision, ante- and post-natal and child health services;
- additional support for families experiencing particular difficulties (to be assessed by the Common Assessment Framework) that mean that children are at risk of poor outcomes;
- further specialist services for children identified as in need, including those in need of protection due to abuse or neglect.

There are different models of Sure Start Children's Centres. Priority was given to setting up the first centres in the 30 per cent most disadvantaged areas. They provided integrated early years provision; parenting, education and family support services; education, training and employment services; health services; and access to wider services. Children's Centres offered 'high intensity' models in these 30 per cent poorest areas. Depending on audits of 'advantage', 'graduated offers' are offered in Sure Start Children's Centres in the remaining 70 per cent of the country. The intention was that a version of the centres would be in 3500 communities by 2010. Much more use was to be made of school facilities – space, resources for leisure and lifelong learning, drop-in health and family support services, etc. – through the extended services agenda throughout the country.

In 2009, key challenges for Children's Centres were identified as doing more to ensure that the most disadvantaged families and children are reached; ensuring that practice was grounded in evidence and would have an impact on improved life chances; and improving arrangements for multi-agency working.

So we return to the theme of this book: multi-professional practice in children's services. It is reassuring that findings from our own small-scale research, the MATCh project, are replicated in the large-scale evaluations of joined-up working initiatives we have reviewed in this final chapter. But before we leave the onion model we need to return to its centre, the outcomes for children, young people, their parents, families and wider communities.

Outcomes for children and young people, their families and communities

What really matters in the reform of public services and the rollout of multi-professional practice is that the delivery of services for children and their families is better than it was, and results in enhanced outcomes for them. The jury is still out on judgements of effectiveness of reforms. But what we do know is that in the UK the trajectory for enhanced life chances is still widening between the rich and poor. Between 22 and 48 months, the attainments and health of young children with the same cognitive skills and physical potential, but with different socio-economic backgrounds, begins to drift apart and by the age of 6 these differential trends are relentlessly set towards adulthood.

The hope is that books like ours will continue the debate about what as a country we can do to address such divisions in the life chances of children, and how as professionals, researchers and policy-makers with responsibility for delivering services, we can play our part in improving them.

Appendix: Multi-agency team checklist

David Cottrell, Angela Anning, Nick Frost, Josephine Green, Mark Robinson

This checklist is derived from the results of the MATCh project exploring the functioning of multi-agency teams. Team members should complete the checklist individually and teams should then discuss the findings collectively. Results may indicate areas of team function that need to be clarified with stakeholder agencies and/or areas of team function that would benefit from more discussion within the team. Where there is divergence of views within a team, members should consider why this is and whether changes to the way the team operates would facilitate team functioning.

Domain 1: Structural: Systems and management	Strongly Disagree/ Never	Disagree/ Sometimes	Agree/ Often	Strongly Agree/ Always
The team has clear objectives that have been agreed by all stakeholding agencies				
The team has clear workload targets that have been agreed by all stake holding agencies				
The team has the authority to make decisions about day-to-day team function (as long as in accord with agreed targets and objectives)				
There is clarity about line management arrangements for all team members				
There are clear mechanisms for coordinating the work of team members				

cont.

Domain 1: Structural: Systems and management (cont.)	Strongly Disagree/ Never	Disagree/ Sometimes	Agree/ Often	Strongly Agree/ Always
Clear mechanisms exist to inform part-time team members about what has taken place in their absence				
Team members are co-located in shared buildings				
Structures exist for communication with all stakeholding agencies (for example, a steering group)				
Stakeholding agencies have made transparent efforts to minimize inequalities caused by different terms and conditions of service for team members employed by different agencies				
Domain 2: Ideological: Sharing and redistributing knowledge/ skills/beliefs				
Different theoretical models are respected within the team				
Different professional groups are accorded equal respect within the team				
Supervision of work is attuned to the needs of the individuals within the team and their various professional backgrounds				
The team encourages members to share skills and ideas with each other				
The team has an awareness of the potential impact of multi-agency working on both professional identity and service users				

cont.

Domain 3: Participation in developing new processes	Strongly Disagree/ Never	Disagree/ Sometimes	Agree/ Often	Strongly Agree/ Always
The team has been able to develop new processes and procedures in order to meet its agreed objectives				
Team members do not necessarily have to follow inappropriate agency of origin procedures where they conflict with agreed team objectives				
Opportunities exist for team members to have time away from the immediacy of delivering services in order to reflect on practice and develop new ways of working (for example, team away days, joint team training events)				
The team engages in joint client-focused activities such as shared assessment and/or consultation with families				
There are regular opportunities for whole team discussion of client-focused activities				
Stakeholding agencies continue to provide ongoing support for the professional development of their staff in multi-agency teams as well as supporting team development activities				

cont.

Domain 4: Inter-professional: Learning through role change	Strongly Disagree/ Never	Disagree/ Sometimes	Agree/ Often	Strongly Agree/ Always
The team has good and clear leadership				
Roles within the team are clear				
The team does not allow certain individuals or professional groups to dominate the team				
The contribution of part-time team members is acknowledged				
The team allows individual members to retain and develop their 'specialist' skills				
Team members are able to learn new ways of practising from each other				

There are no right answers but teams where most members tend to agree with the statements above are likely to function more efficiently and effectively.

Bibliography

Ancona, D., Malone, T.W., Orlikowski, W.J., and Senge, P.M. (2007) In praise of the incomplete leader, *Harvard Business Review*, February, pp. 94–9.

Anning, A. and Ball, M. (2008) *Improving Children's Services*. London: Sage Publications Ltd.

Argyris, C. and Schön, D.A. (1976) *Theory in Practice*. San Francisco: Jossey-Bass.

Atkinson, M., Jones, M., Lamont, E. (2007) *Multi-agency Working and its Implications for Practice: A Review of the Literature*. London: CfBT, Education Trust.

Atkinson, M., Wilkin, A., Scott, A. and Kinder, K. (2001) *Multi-Agency Activity: An Audit of Activity, Local Government Association Research, Report 17*. Slough: National Foundation for Education and Research.

ATL (Association of Teachers and Lecturers) (2003) *Raising Standards and Tackling the Workload*. London: DfES.

Audit Commission (1996) *Misspent Youth*. London: Audit Commission.

Audit Commission (2004) *Youth Justice 2004: A Review of the Reformed Youth Justice System*. London: Audit Commission.

Balls, E. (2007) Disabled children must stay top of the agenda, *Community Care*, 6 December, p. 23.

Bax, M. and Whitmore, K. (1991) District handicap teams in England: 1983–8, *Archives of Disease in Childhood*, 66: 656–64.

Belsky, J., Barnes, J. and Melhuish, E. (eds) (2007) *The National Evaluation of Sure Start: Does Area-based Early Intervention Work?* Bristol: The Policy Press.

Bilson, A. (ed.) (2005) *Evidence-based Practice in Social Work*. London: Whiting & Birch.

Bradbury, H., Frost, N., Kilminster, S. and Zukas, M. (2010) *Beyond Reflective Practice*. London: Routledge.

Bronfenbrenner, U. (1979) *The Ecology of Human Development: Experiments by Nature and Design*. Cambridge, MA: Harvard University Press.

BSRM/RCP (2003) *Rehabilitation Following Brain Injury: National Clinical Guidelines*. London: Royal College of Physicians.

Cabinet Office, (2006) *Reading Out: An Action Plan on Social Exclusion.* London: Cabinet Office Social Exclusion Task Force.

Cameron, A. and Lart, R. (2003) Factors promoting and obstacles hindering joint working: a systematic review of the research evidence, *Journal of Integrated Care*, 11(2).

Castells, M. (1998) *The End of the Millennium.* Oxford: Blackwell.

Children and Society (2009) Special issue: the outcomes of integrated working for children and young people.

Cottrell, D. and Kramm, A. (2005) Growing Up? A History of CAMHS (1987–2005), *Child and Adolescent Mental Health*, 10(3): 111–17.

Cross, M. (2006) A spineless performance, *Guardian*, Thursday 12 January.

Dartington Social Research Unit (2004) *Refocusing Children's Services toward Prevention: Lessons from the Literature* (DfES Research Report 510). London: DfES [online]. Available: http://www.dfes.gov.uk/research/data/upload files/RR510.pdf.

DCSF (Department for Children, Schools and Families) (2007a) *The Children's Plan.* London: DCSF.

DCSF (Department for Children, Schools and Families) (2007b) *Aiming Higher for Disabled Children.* London: DCSF.

DCSF (Department for Children, Schools and Families) (2007c) *Care Matters: A Time for Change.* London: DCSF.

DCSF (Department for Children, Schools and Families) (2008a) *Aiming High for Young People.* London: DCSF.

DCSF (Department for Children, Schools and Families) (2008b) *Children's Trusts: Statutory Guidance.* London: DCSF.

DCSF (Department for Children, Schools and Families) (2008c) *The 21st Century School: A Transformation in Education.* London: DCSF.

DCSF (Department for Children, Schools and Families) (2008d) *Care Matters: Time to Deliver for Children in Care.* London: DCSF.

DCSF (Department for Children, Schools and Families) (2008e) *Building Brighter Futures: Next Steps for the Children's Workforce.* London: DCSF.

DCSF/DoH (Department for Children, Schools and Families/Department of Health) (2008) *Children and Young People in Mind: The Final Report of the National CAMHS Review.* London: DCSF.

DES (Department of Education and Science) (1978) *The Report of the Committee of Enquiry into the Education of Handicapped Children and Young People* (The Warnock Report). London: HMSO.

DETR (Department of the Environment, Transport and Regions) (1999) *Modernising Local Government: Guidance for the Local Government Act 1999, Best Value.* London: DETR.

DfES (Department for Education and Skills) (2001) *Special Educational Needs Code of Practice.* Nottingham: DfES.

DfES (Department for Education and Skills) (2003) *Every Child Matters*. London: HMSO.

DfES (Department for Education and Skills) (2004) *Every Child Matters: Change for Children*. London: HMSO.

DfES (Department for Education and Skills) (2005) *Youth Matters*. London: HMSO.

DfES (Department for Education and Skills) (2006) *Care Matters: Transforming the Lives of Children and Young People in Care*. London: HMSO.

DfES/DoH (Department for Education and Skills/Department of Health) (2002a) *Together from the Start: Practical Guidance for Professionals Working with Disabled Children (0–2) and their Families*. London: HMSO.

DfES/DoH (Department for Education and Skills/Department of Health) (2002b) *Developing Early Intervention/Support Services for Deaf Children and their Families*. London: HMSO.

DfES/DoH (Department for Education and Skills/Department of Health) (2004a) *The National Framework for Children, Young People and Maternity Services*. London: DoH.

DfES/DoH (Department for Education and Skills/Department of Health) (2004b) *Acquired Brain Injury*. London: Department of Health.

DoH (Department of Health) (1976) *Fit for the Future: Report of the Committee on Child Health Services* (The Court Report, Cmnd 6684, vol. 1). London: HMSO.

DoH (Department of Health) (2001) *Hospital Episode Statistics, 2000/2001*. London: DoH.

DoH (Department of Health) (2005) *Commissioning a Patient-led NHS*. London: DoH.

DoH (Department of Health) (2008a) *Child Health Strategy*, London: DoH.

DoH (Department of Health) (2008b) *High Quality Care for All: NHS Next Stage Review, Darsi Report*. London: DoH.

DoH/DCSF (Department of Health/Department for Children, Schools and Families) (2008) *The Child Health Promotion Programme*. London: DoH.

Edwards, A. and Fox, C. (2005) Using activity theory to evaluate a complex response to social exclusion, *Educational and Child Psychology*, 22(1): 50–61.

Engestrom, Y. (ed.) (1999) *Perspectives on Activity Theory*. New York: Cambridge University Press.

Engestrom, Y. (2000) Making expansive decisions: an activity theoretical study of practitioners building collaborative medical care for children, in K.M. Allwood and M. Selart (eds) *Creative Decision Making in the Social World*. Amsterdam: Kluwer.

Engestrom, Y. (2001) Expansive learning at work: toward an activity theoretical reconceptualization, *Journal of Education and Work*, 14(1): 133–56.

Engestrom, Y., Engestrom, R. and Vahaaho, T. (1999) When the center does not hold: the importance of knotworking, in S. Chaiklin, M. Hedegaard and U. Jensen (eds) *Activity Theory and Social Practice*. Aarhus: Aarhus University Press.

Eraut, M. (1999) Non-formal learning in the workplace: The hidden dimension of lifelong learning. A framework for analysis and the problems it poses for researchers. Paper presented at the First International Conference on Researching Work and Learning, University of Leeds.

Farmakopoulou, N. (2002) 'What lies underneath?' An inter-organisational analysis of collaboration between education and social work, *British Journal of Social Work*, 32(8).

Frost, N. (2001) Professionalism, change and the politics of lifelong learning, *Studies in Continuing Education*, 23(1): 5–17.

Frost, N. (2005) *Professionalism, Partnership and Joined Up Thinking*. Dartington: Research in Practice.

Frost, N. and Lloyd, A. (2006) Implementing multi-disciplinary teamwork in the new child welfare policy environment, *Journal of Integrated Care*, 14: 2.

Frost, N. and Parton, N. (2009) *Understanding Children's Social Care*. London: Sage.

Garrett, L. and Lodge, S. (2009) *Integrated Practice on the Front Line*. Dartington: Research in Practice.

Garrett, P.M. (2005) Social work's 'electronic turn', *Critical Social Policy*, 25(4): 529–53.

Glass, N. (1999) Sure Start: the development of an early intervention programme for young children in the UK, *Children & Society*, 13: 257–64.

Glisson, C. and Hemmelgarn, A. (1998) The effects of organizational climate and interorganizational coordination on the quality and outcomes of children's service systems, *Child Abuse and Neglect*, 22(5): 401–21.

Government Chief Social Researcher's Office (2005) *Trying It Out: The Role of 'Pilots' in Policy-Making*. London: Cabinet Office.

Granville, J. and Langton, P. (2002) Working across boundaries: systemic and psychodynamic perspectives on multi-disciplinary and inter-agency practice, *Journal of Social Work Practice*, 16(1): 23–7.

Greenberg, D. and Shroder, M. (1997) *The Digest of Social Experiments*, 2nd edn. Washington, DC: Urban Institute Press.

Hall, D. (1997) Child development teams: are they fulfilling their purpose? *Child: Care, Health and Development*, 23: 87–99.

Harré, R. (1983) *Personal Being*. Oxford: Blackwell.

Haywood, J. (2005) Vision and the challenges ahead, *Partners*, 41: 2–3.

Home Office (1998) *Interdepartmental Circular on Establishing Youth Offending Teams*, 22 December. London: Home Office.

Home Office (2000) *Report of Policy Action Team 12: Young People*. London: HMSO.

Hudson, B. (2002) Interprofessionality in health and social care: the Achilles' heel of partnership, *Journal of Interprofessional Care*, 16(1).

Jamieson, A. and Owen, S. (2000) *Ambition for Change: Partnerships, Children and Work*. London: National Children's Bureau.

Jenkins, R. (2002) *Social Identity*. London: Routledge.

Jenks, C. (1996) *Childhood*. London: Routledge.

Kay, A. and Teasdale, G. (2001) Head injury in the United Kingdom, *World Journal of Surgery*, 25: 1210–20.

Laming, H. (2003) *The Victoria Climbié Inquiry*. London: HMSO.

Laming, H. (2009) *The Protection of Children in England: A Progress Report*. London: TSO.

Lave, J. and Wenger, E. (1991) *Situated Learning: Legitimate Peripheral Participation*. Cambridge: Cambridge University Press.

Loxley, A. (1997) *Collaboration in Health and Welfare: Working in Difference*. London: Jessica Kingsley.

Miller, C. and McNicholl, A. (2003) *Integrating Children's Services: Issues and Practice*. London: Office of Public Management.

NECF (National Evaluation of Children's Fund) (2004) *Developing Collaboration in Preventative Services for Children and Young People: The First Annual Report of NECF*. London: DfES.

NECT (National Evaluation of Children's Trusts) (2005) *Realising Children's Trust Arrangements: The Full Phase 1 Report*. London: DfES.

NECTP (2007) *Children's Trusts Pathfinders: Innovative Partnerships for Improving the Wellbeing of Children*. London: DfES.

NESS (National Evaluation of Sure Start) (2004) *Implementing Sure Start Local Programmes: Full Report, Part 1 and Part 2*. London: HMSO.

NESS (National Evaluation of Sure Start) (2005a) *Early Impacts of Sure Start Local Programmes on Children and Families*, Report 013. London: HMSO.

NESS (National Evaluation of Sure Start) (2005b) *Implementing Sure Start Local Programmes: An Integrated Overview of the First Four Years*. London: HMSO.

NESS (National Evaluation of Sure Start) (2005c) *Variation in Sure Start Local Programme Effectiveness: Early Preliminary Findings*, Report 014. London: HMSO.

NESS (National Evaluation of Sure Start) (2005d) *Report on the Case Studies of the Implementation Module: National Evaluation of Sure Start*. London: HMSO.

NESS (National Evaluation of Sure Start) (2008) *The Impact of Sure Start Local Programmes on Three Year Olds and Their Families*. London: HMSO.

NHS, HAS (National Health Service, Health Advisory Service) (1995) *Child & Adolescent Mental Health Services: Together We Stand*. London: HAS.

NICE (National Institute for Clinical Excellence) (2003) *Head Injury: Triage, Assessment, Investigation and Early Management of Head Injury in Infants, Children and Adolescents*. London: NICE.

Ofsted (2009a) *Comprehensive Area Assessment: Annual Rating of Council Children's Services for 2009*. London: Ofsted.

Ofsted (2009b) *Unannounced Inspections of Contact, Referral and Assessment*. London: Ofsted.

Ofsted (2009c) *Inspections of Safeguarding and Looked after Children Services*, London: Ofsted.

Øvretveit, J. (1993) *Coordinating Community Care: Multidisciplinary Teams and Care Management*. Buckingham: Open University Press.

Percy-Smith, J. (2005) *What Works in Strategic Partnership Working for Children*. Barkingside: Barnardo's.

Petrioni, P. (1994) Inter-professional teamwork: its history and development in hospitals, general practice and community care (UK), in A. Leathard (ed.) *Going Inter-professional: Working together for Health and Welfare*. London: Routledge.

Power, M. (1997) *The Audit Society: Rituals of Verification*. Oxford: Oxford University Press.

Puonti, A. (2004) Learning to work together: collaboration between authorities in economic-crime investigation. PhD thesis, University of Helsinki.

Robinson, M., Atkinson, M. and Downing, D. (2008) *Supporting Theory Building in Integrated Services Research*. Slough: National Foundation for Educational Research.

Robinson, M., Anning, A. and Frost, N. (2005) 'When is a teacher not a teacher?' Knowledge creation and the professional identity of teachers in multi-agency settings, *Studies in Continuing Education*, 27(2): 175–91.

Shatzman, L. (1991) Dimensional analysis: notes on an alternative approach to the grounding of theory in qualitative research, in D. Maines (ed.) *Social Organisation and Social Process*. New York: Aldine.

Sheldon Report (1968) *Child Welfare Centres, Public Health*, 82: 52–4.

Sims, D., Fineman, S. and Gabriel, Y. (1993) *Organising and Organisations: An Introduction*. London: Sage.

Skelcher, D., Mathur, N. and Smith, M. (2004) *Effective Partnership and Good Governance: Lessons for Policy and Practice*. Birmingham: INLOGOV.

Strauss, A.L. and Corbin, J. (1998) *Basics of Qualitative Research: Techniques and Procedures for Developing Grounded Theory*. London: Sage.

Thornhill, S., Teasedale, G.M., Murray, G.D., McEwen, J., Roy, C.W. and Penny, K.I. (2000) Disability in young people and adults one year after head injury: prospective cohort study, *British Medical Journal*, 320: 1631–5.

UNICEF (2007) *Child Poverty in Perspective: An Overview of Child Well Being in Rich Countries*. Florence: UNICEF Innocenti Research Centre.

Wall, K. (2003) *Special Needs and Early Years*. London: Paul Chapman.

Warmington, P., Daniels, H., Edwards, A., Brown, S., Leadbetter, J., Martin, D. and Middleton, D. (2004) *TLRPIII: Learning in and for Interagency*

Working. Interagency Collaboration: A Review of the Literature. Birmingham: University of Birmingham.

Watson, D., Townsley, R. and Abbot, D. (2002) Exploring multi-agency working in services to disabled children with complex health care needs and their families, *Journal of Clinical Nursing*, 11(3): 367–75.

Wenger, E. (1998) *Communities of Practice.* Cambridge: Cambridge University Press.

Whalley, M. and the Pen Green Centre Team (1997) *Involving Parents in their Children's Learning.* London: Paul Chapman.

Wheatley, H. (2006) *Pathways to Success.* London: The Council for Disabled Children.

Young, K., Ashby, D., Boaz, A. and Grayson, L. (2002) Social science and the evidence-based policy movement, *Social Policy and Society*, 1(3): 215–24.

Zahir, M. and Bennet, S. (1994) Review of child development teams, *Archives of Disease in Childhood*, 70: 224–8.

Index

accountability, 3, 27, 29, 69
  clear lines of, 103–4
  professional, 71
  team types, 27–30
activity theory, 11–2, 84
Aiming Higher for Disabled Children, 45
Aiming Higher for Young People, 112
apprenticeship style of learning, 76
Argyris, C., 53
assessment of children and young people,
  124–6
  joint assessments, 82
assessment for qualifications, 77
Atkinson, M., 10
Audit Commission, 32, 105–6, 116–17
autonomy, 66–8
away days, 48, 81, 134
Aysnley-Green, A., 115

'Baby Peter', 7, 116, 120
Balls, E., 44, 115
barriers to multi-professional working,
  71
  addressing status and hierarchical barriers,
  106
Birkbeck College, 127
Blair, T., 3, 111
Bolton, 99
boundary disputes, 65, 70
boundary objects, 83–4
'boundary spanning' individuals, 105
British Society of Rehabilitation Medicine
  (BSRM), 41
Bronfenbrenner, U., 128
Building Brighter Futures, 118

Care Matters, 113
Care Services Improvement Partnership
  (CSIP), 117
Castells, M., 103
checklist, 132–5
child and adolescent mental health
  practitioners (CAMHPs), 32–5, 73–4

*Child and Adolescent Mental Health Services:
  Together We Stand*, 32
child and adolescent mental health (CAMH)
  teams, 32–5
  see also young people's team
child development team, 43–6
  local practice, 45–6
  models of understanding, 52–9
  national policy, 43–5
  sharing knowledge and expertise, 81–3
Child Health Promotion Package, 6
childhood, 5–6, 51–9, 112
Children Act 1989, 4, 109
Children Act, 2004, 4–7, 47, 61, 94, 102, 107,
  111, 116, 123
Children and Young People in Mind, 5
Children's Centres, 4–6, 35, 98, 107, 111,
  119, 122, 129–30
Children's Fund, 10, 35, 120–2
Children's Plan, 6–7, 37, 44
Children's Rights Alliance for England
  (CREA), 126
Children's Trusts, 94, 111, 116, 122–3
Children's Workforce Development Council
  (CWDC), 8, 78, 107, 117–18
classroom support workers, 118
clients *see* service users
Climbié, Victoria, 107
codified knowledge, 76–8
collaboration, 7
co-location, 102–4, 107, 127
Commissioning a Patient-led NHS, 124
Common Assessment Framework (CAF), 104,
  125–7, 130
common way of working, negotiating, 21
communication structures, 107
communities of practice, 11–12, 51, 59, 61,
  64
complementary models, 52–9
conditions of service, 104–5
confidentiality, 16, 19, 20–1, 25, 70, 91, 98–9,
  125–6
Contact Point, 127

cooperation, 7
coordinated team, 27–8, 32
coordination, 7
core and extended team, 28
Court Report, 43
Crime and Disorder Act 1998, 31
critical incident diaries, 15, 19–20
critical incidents, 15, 19–20, 84, 89, 101
　see also dilemmas; vignette scenarios

data collection methods, 13–26
Development Agency (IdeA), 117
dilemmas, 89–101
　common to multi-professional teams, 93
　ideological, 96–8
　inter-professional, 100
　procedural, 98–100
　structural, 93–6
　see also critical incidents
disabilities, children with, 35–45
　see also child development team; nursery
　　team
dominant models, 52–9

education, 22–5, 30–2, 35–7, 64, 72, 95, 97,
　100, 119, 127
　see also nursery team; special schools
Edwards, A., 121
employment
　pay and service conditions, 104
Engestrom. Y., 12, 83–4
Eraut, M., 77
ethics, 21, 25, 70, 82, 91
ethnicity, 32, 38
Every Child Matters, 4–7, 61, 99, 107, 111–12,
　114, 116, 124–7
Every Child Matters: Change for Children, 4
evidence-based reform, 9, 40
evidence of joint working, 19, 113
expansive learning, 12, 84
extended schools, 5, 122

Family Nurse Partnerships, 6
Farmakopoulou, N., 109
fieldnotes, 17
focus groups, 20–5
front-line delivery, integrated, 127–30
Frost, N., 8, 70
fully managed teams, 27–8, 30, 32, 35, 38

Glisson, C., 113
governance, integrated, 115–16

Granville, J., 85

head injury team, 29–30, 40–3
　local practice, 41–3
　models of understanding, 52–5
　national policy, 40–1
Hemmelgarn, A., 113
Hudson, B., 71
humour, 80, 82

implementation of integrated services,
　111–31
　integrated front-line delivery, 127–30
　integrated processes, 124–7
　integrated strategy, 120–4
　inter-agency governance, 115–16
　'onion', 114–15, 122, 130
　outcomes for service users, their families
　　and communities, 9–10, 108, 133, 185
　statutory inspections, 116–17
　workforce reform, 117–20
information sharing
　integrated processes, 126–7
inspections, statutory, 116–17
integrated front-line delivery, 127–30
integrated processes, 122
integrated strategy, 120–4
inter-agency governance, 115–16
inter-professional checklist, 132–5
interviews, 15–19
　analysis of, 19

jargon, 20, 22, 80, 90–1, 106
Jerkins, R., 12
joint accountability team, 29, 30, 45
joint client-focused activities, 109
joint enterprise, 11, 83, 106, 108
joint procedural work, 103

Kay, A., 40
key worker, 83, 95
knotworking model, 84, 121
knowledge
　creating new forms of, 76–86
　nature of professional knowledge, 8–12,
　　17–20, 54, 74
　sharing *see* sharing knowledge and
　　expertise, 133, 76–86

Labour Party, 3–4, 43, 69, 113–15
　see also policy

Laming Report, 7, 107
Langton, P., 85
Lave, J., 76
leadership, 93, 102, 103, 105, 115–16, 122,
    129, 135
learning
    apprenticeship style, 76
    teams learning together, 11–12, 76–86, 135
line management, 38, 45, 104, 115
local authorities
    statutory inspections of services, 116–17
local practice
    child development team, 44–5
    head injury team, 41–2
    nursery team, 37–8
    young people's team, 34–5
    youth crime team, 31–2
Loxley, A., 71

management *see* organization and
    management
MATCh project, 51, 59, 61, 77, 79–80, 89, 99,
    103, 105, 111
    theoretical frameworks, 11–12
McNicholl, A., 102
medical model, 54–5
meetings *see* team meetings
MENCAP, 39
Miller, C., 102
Misspent Youth, 31
models of understanding, 51–9
Morris, E., 118
mutual engagement, 11

National Collaborating Centre for Acute
    Care, 40
National College for School Leadership (later
    National College for Leadership of
    Schools and Children's Services), 120
National Evaluation of the Children's Fund
    (NECF), 10, 120–2
National Evaluation of Sure Start (NESS) local
    programmes, 4, 98, 127–9
*National Framework for Children, Young People
    and Maternity Services*, 5, 41, 115
National Health Care Record initiative, 125
National Health Service (NHS), 6, 33, 38–9,
    44–5, 124–5
    information technology, 119
National Institute for Clinical Excellence
    (NICE), 40, 120

national policy *see* policy
National Professional Qualification in
    Integrated Centre Leadership (NPQICL),
    120
National Service Framework (NSF), 41
needs-based model, 55–6
New Labour, 3–7, 43
nursery team, 39–40
    local practice, 39–40
    models of understanding, 52, 55–6
    national policy, 37–9

observations of team meetings, 62–6
Office for Standards in Education (Ofsted),
    116–17
'onion' of integrated services, 114
organization and management
    challenge of managing multi-professional
        teamwork, 45–8
    checklist, 132–5
    child development team, 43–5
    head injury team, 40–3
    nursery team, 35–9
    young people's team, 32–5
    youth crime team, 31–2
organizational climate, 94
Øvretveit, J., 27, 46, 48

part-time staff, 95, 108, 133
pay and conditions of service, 104–5
Pen Green Centre, 120
peripheral and core team members, 74, 108
    acknowledging peripheral members, 74
personal/professional dilemmas, 10, 15, 17,
    20–5, 89–101
policy
    child development team, 43–4
    head injury team, 40–1
    nursery team, 35–7
    young people's team, 32–4
    youth crime team, 31–2
policy-making and service delivery strategies
    acknowledging peripheral team members,
        74–5, 94, 102, 108
    acknowledging professional diversity, 102,
        108
    awareness of impact of change on service
        users, 102, 108
    clear lines of accountability, 102–4
    co-location of service deliveries, 102,
        107–8

employment conditions, 102, 104–5
joint client-focused activities, 102, 109
joint procedural work and inclusive
  planning systems, 102, 103
leadership vision, 102, 105
role clarity and sense of purpose, 102,
  105–6
shared objectives and aims, 102, 106–7
specialist skills retention, 102, 109
status and hierarchical barriers, 102,
  106
support for professional development, 102,
  109
transparent communication structures,
  102, 107
Portage home visitor scheme, 24, 38
practice manager, 64–5
procedures, 2, 42, 67–8, 70, 98–9, 103
professional development
  ongoing support for, 109
professional diversity, acknowledging, 108
professional identity, 50–7
professional knowledge
  nature, 51–9, 76–86
professional supervision/support, 35, 45, 48,
  62, 64, 66, 69, 76, 81, 94, 100, 104, 123,
  133
professionalism, 70–5
Puonti, A., 78

qualifications, 73, 76–8, 118, 120

Raising Standards and Tackling the Workload,
  119
Ready, Steady, Change, 126
Reaching Out, 6
record-keeping, 69, 91, 99, 124–5
reflective practice, 25
reification, 11, 15, 17, 48, 83, 98, 103
research methods
  choice of teams for study, 13–26, 16
  critical incident diaries, 15, 19–20
  data collection, 14
  ethics and confidentiality, 25
  focus groups, 20
  interviews, 15, 17–19
  phases of the research, 16
  validation event, 24–6
roles, 60–75
  role clarity, 105–6
Royal College of Physicians (RCP), 41

Royal College of Surgeons, 41
Royal Society for Mentally Handicapped
  Children and Adults (MENCAP), 27, 39

The Scaled Approach, 31–2
scenarios, 20–4
Schön, D.A., 53
service users, 51, 102, 126, 133
  awareness of impact of change on, 108
  impact of multi-professional practices on
    outcomes for, 108, 133
  and labels for professionals, 51, 56, 58
shared aims/objectives, 106–7
sharing knowledge and expertise, 76–86
  consensus and conflict as catalyst for
    learning, 83–5
  formal exchanges, 80–4
  how knowledge and expertise is shared,
    78–9
  ideological dilemmas, 96–8
  informal exchange, 79–80
  tension between sharing expertise and
    acknowledging specialist expertise, 20–1
Shatzman, L., 19
Sheldon Report, 43
Shroder, M., 9
Sims, D., 70
Skelcher, D., 105
social construction, 51–9
social deprivation, 67–70
social events, 80
social exclusion, 121, 128
Social Exclusion Unit Policy Action Team,
  121
social model, 56–7
Society of British Neurological Surgeons,
  41
Special Educational Needs Code of Practice, 38
special schools, 35
specialists
  paying attention to specialist skills
    retention, 109
  recognizing specialisms within a team, 109
status, 70–5, 76, 97, 102
  addressing barriers related to, 107
strategic objectives, agreed, 107–8
Sure Start, 4, 8, 127–30
  evaluation of, 4
systems
  approach to understanding, 52–4
  complex hierarchy of, 52

tacit knowledge, 76
teaching assistants, 72, 119
team-building, 21, 42, 48
team culture, 48, 60–75
team meetings
  observations of, 15–17, 62–6
  sharing knowledge and expertise, 60–75,
    81–3
team types, 27–48
theory in action, 51–60
Third Way, 3
training
  teams training together, 109

user choice
  see also service users

validation event, 24–5
videotaping assessments, 82–4
vignette scenarios, 89–93

Warmington, P., 10, 85
Warnock Report, 38

Wenger, E., 11–12, 15, 51, 59, 61, 64, 76, 80,
  83, 98, 106–7
work location
  co-location, 102, 104, 107, 127
workforce reform, 117–18
workloads, deployment of, 64, 94–6

Young, K., 9
young people's team, 33–6, 67–70
  local practice, 34–5
  models of understanding, 67–70
  national policy, 33–4
  sharing knowledge and expertise,
    67–70
youth crime team, 31–3, 62–6
  local practice, 33
  models of understanding, 67–70
  national policy, 31
  roles, 31–2
Youth Justice Board, 32
Youth Matters, 112
Youth Offending Service, 105
youth work, 67, 112, 118

Related books from Open University Press

Purchase from www.openup.co.uk or order through your local bookseller

---

MULTIPROFESSIONAL COMMUNICATION
MAKING SYSTEMS WORK FOR CHILDREN

Georgina Glenny and Caroline Roaf

2009 NASEN Award Winner!

- What are the features of successful multiprofessional work?
- How can schools, local authorities and individual fieldworkers work effectively to achieve the best possible outcomes for the children and families with whom they are working?
- How can the Every Child Matters policy agenda be implemented successfully?

This book examines a series of case studies of multiprofessional work, in order to understand what works and why. In the successful case studies, the fieldworkers were able to reflect on the organisational contexts in which they were operating. This was achieved through a carefully managed series of feedback loops, which ensured that good quality information was shared at all levels. With an effective communication system in place they could resolve difficulties and evolve new ways of working together to improve their joint practice.

Multiprofessional Communication is important reading for students on courses with a focus on multiprofessional working, as well as practitioners and policy makers in Education, Health and Social Care.

Contents
List of figures and tables – Acknowledgements – Introduction – The challenge of multi-professional working – The research base: exploring multiprofessional communication systems in action – Evolving a communication system – Customizing provision to meet local needs – Achieving a positive problem solving culture – The importance of relation-ships in the field – Conclusions: the dynamics of complexity – References – Index.

2008   152pp
978–0–335–22856–0 (Paperback)   978–0–335–22855–3 (Hardback)

'TRANSFORMING' CHILDREN'S SERVICES
SOCIAL WORK, NEOLIBERALISM AND THE MODERN WORLD

Paul Michael Garrett

This book provides an accessible overview of the 'transformation' of Children's Services in England. In doing this, it draws on social theory, critical social policy and takes account of developments in other countries.

Paul Michael Garrett argues that the many changes which have taken place within, and beyond, Children's Services are related to the politics of Neoliberalism which, it is maintained, lie at the core of the *Change for Children* programme.

Readers will find detailed discussion on:

- The Laming Report which examined the death of Victoria Climbié
- The case of 'Baby P'
- Social work's 'electronic turn' and the use of ICTs in Children's Services
- Controversial plans to introduce *Contactpoint* (a database on all children)
- More pervasive patterns of surveillance
- How 'ASBO politics' has influenced the 'transformation' agenda
- So-called 'Problem Families' and the measures put in place to respond to such families
- Controversial plans to set up 'Social Work Practices' for children in public care

'Transforming' Children's Services will be a vital text for social work and social policy students. Furthermore, the book directly addresses a range of issues of direct concern to practitioners.

Contents
Introduction – Theorizing Neoliberal 'Transformation' – The 'transformational reform agenda': The Change for Children programme – Neoliberal Globalism, 'Race' and Place: Reviewing the Laming Report on the death of Victoria Climbié – Making 'Anti-Social Behaviour': ASBO Politics – 'Problem Families' and 'Sinbin' Solutions – Making 'happier' children and more 'fulfilled' social workers? Privatizing social work services for 'looked after' children – Conclusion – Notes – References

2009   200pp
978–0–335–23425–7 (Paperback)   978–0–335–23424–0 (Hardback)

EARLY CHILDHOOD STUDIES
A MULTIPROFESSIONAL PERSPECTIVE
Liz Jones, Rachel Holmes and John Powell

A celebration of the tremendous strides made towards the achievement of a multiprofessional early years workforce, and a challenge to those responsible for training the next generation of professionals. . . Students and trainers, policy makers and practitioners have a duty to be knowledgeable, to be able to reflect on their beliefs and practice and to articulate concerns, share their views, convey their enthusiasm and act as advocates for young children. This book will help them do just that.

Lesley Abbott OBE, Manchester Metropolitan University

Early Childhood Studies critically engages the reader in issues that relate to young children and their lives from a multiprofessional perspective. Whilst offering a theoretically rigorous treatment of issues relating to early childhood studies, the book also provides practical discussion of strategies that could inform multiprofessional practice. It draws upon case studies to help the reader make practical sense of theoretical ideas and develop a critical and reflective attitude. Hard and pressing questions are asked so that beliefs, ideas, views and assumptions about notions of the child and childhood are constantly critiqued and reframed for the post-modern world.

The first part of the book explores the early years, power and politics by looking at child rights, the politics of play, families, and working with parents and carers. The second part explores facts and fantasies about childhood experiences, such as anti-discriminatory practice, the law, child protection, and health issues. The final section encourages the reader to explore what childhood means from historical, ideological and cultural perspectives, and looks at how popular assumptions arise.

This is a key critical text for early childhood students, academics and researchers, as well as practitioners who want to develop their reflective practice.

Contents
List of Contributors – Foreword – Preface and acknowledgements – Introduction – Part 1: Power, politics and childhood – Researching young children within a multiprofessional perspective – Exploring tensions within the interplay of rights, duties and responsibilities – The politics of play – Exploring families – Working with parents and carers – Part 2: Working together: Facts, frameworks and fantasies – Multiprofessional perspectives – Anti-discriminatory practice – Legal issues – Child protection – Integration, inclusion and diversity – Health in childhood – Part 3: Children's childhoods – Exploring representations of children and childhood in history and film: Silencing a voice that is already blue in the face from shouting – Exploring representations of children and childhood in photography and documentary: Visualizing the silence – International perspectives – Understanding development – Concluding remarks – Index.

2005   240pp
978–0–335–21485–3 (Paperback)   978–0–335–21486–0 (Hardback)